# On the Verge

# On the Verge

*Chronicle of a walk along the verge of SH1 from Bluff to Cape Reinga, in support of Mental Health: October-November 2021.*

Roger Leslie

| Library of Congress Control Number: | | 2024919034 |
|---|---|---|
| ISBN: | Hardcover | 978-1-6698-8187-2 |
| | Softcover | 978-1-6698-8186-5 |
| | eBook | 978-1-6698-8185-8 |

Print information available on the last page.

Rev. date: 09/10/2024

**To order additional copies of this book, contact:**
Xlibris
NZ TFN: 0800 008 756 (Toll Free inside the NZ)
NZ Local: 9-801 1905 (+64 9801 1905 from outside New Zealand)
www.Xlibris.co.nz
Orders@Xlibris.co.nz
862489

# CONTENTS

# Preface

A small boy sat gazing out the window of the school classroom. He was six years old and to him the window was more than a source of light or fresh air, it was the portal to another world. A world that was much more exciting than the things on offer in his immediate environment. He didn't hate the school, but he hated being at school. He chafed at the restriction it imposed on him and he wasn't a good fit in the learning model that the education system seemed to be based on. He was constantly in trouble for inattention and daydreaming.

He had mild dyslexia, and struggled to interpret the intended meaning of printed words and form numbers into the groups everyone else thought were correct. He wondered if he would ever conform to their expectations. He smiled to himself at the thought that out the window somewhere there might just be a world that had an opening for dreamers like him.

In the muted distance he heard his name and noticed all the other kids were looking at him. The teacher was trying to get his attention. She was holding up a book. "Roger, as I was telling the others, this book is about a man walking from North Cape to Bluff. For homework over the weekend, I'd like you to write a story about where you'd like to walk, and why. Over the next week or so I'm going to read to you some parts of the book. I'm sure you'll find it interesting." This piqued his curiosity and for once the word 'homework' didn't dim his attention.

He hurried home and wanted to get started on the story straight away. His mother wondered if he was 'sickening for something' as he usually didn't get on to weekend homework until bedtime Sunday evening, if at all. He was much happier digging an underground hut or climbing to the swaying heights of the macrocarpa trees that lined the road boundary of his home. She mentioned the unusual enthusiasm for the homework task at the tea table. His father paused mid mouthful and looked at him. He didn't say anything, he just looked.

The boy wasn't always sure what his father thought about stuff like this. He suspected his father was no lover of school either and maybe, just maybe, buried under the responsibility of feeding his large family in lean times, he was a dreamer too. The boy told the family of the man who walked from North Cape to Bluff. He was bursting to tell them that he would do the same thing one day himself, but he'd learned to keep most of his crazy ideas to himself. It seemed to him that all the cool things he wanted to do were forbidden by someone. He took the risk of family ridicule and asked

'Who is allowed to do something like that?'

His father surprised him by replying, 'Anyone is, you just need a lot of determination and a good pair of boots!'

'Even me?' 'Even you.'

The hubbub of the family meal conversation receded into silence in his mind, and he could clearly see an older version of himself setting off 'in a good pair of boots'.

This vision would stay with him for 60 years. This is that story.

# Day 1

## Bluff to Invercargill

The dream to walk from Bluff to Cape Reinga solidified when, in 2008, I starting walking in a more serious way. I entered walking events and loved them. I particularly loved the mountain and off-road races. Until 2008, I had never done a marathon, not even a half-marathon. In fact, any sentence with the word marathon in it, caused a certain curl of lip in my mental demeanour. Who did these marathons anyway? Crazy people, the lot of them.

Then a casual throw-away comment from my doctor about walking, to overcome sciatic pain, plunged me into the world of running and walking great distances for fun. In that world I found the people were great. They were invariably fun people. They enjoyed each other, and when the word 'endurance' entered a conversation, their heads would snap up, and light would glint in their eyes. I found that almost anyone could join this group, and be accepted without question into its embrace. After my first half marathon, I was hooked. Soon full marathons followed and they in turn weren't enough. I never learned to enjoy running. I was a walker, but when one walks far enough the advantages of running are threadbare.

Back in 1978 I married Joy, and from then onwards, the things I did, especially the crazy things, impacted her. She had freely vowed to stick with me through thick and thin, hard times and easy, and more pertinently, for better or worse. I suspect she hadn't calculated that the 'worse' part, might involve freezing by some remote mountain path in the middle of the night, waiting to offer support and succour to her mad husband, as he wandered by. (This is discussed in more detail in the Wild Side, Appendix One). Over the years I had mentioned that one day I would walk the length of the country, But I'm not sure that she gave this any more consideration than any of the other ideas I had from time to time.

The loose plan in the back of my mind was to do this when I retired from fulltime work, but before I got too old and decrepit to do it. She certainly started to notice the increase in the number of times the great walk was mentioned, and in the seriousness of them. I gave her the choice of opting out, although she may dispute that, and asked her if she wanted to be the main support person for the whole trip? She said, words to the effect, of course I will.

## Preparation

I wanted to do it for myself, but I also wanted to make it meaningful, so I chose to support, and raise funds for, the mental health agency ABLE. With the help of my daughter-in-law Sarah, we set up a give- a-little page and a dedicated page on Facebook, called Walkable. We purchased a camper van, in the form of an old converted DAF ambulance, with the Rover 3.5 V8 motor. I took it to be serviced and pointed out my intention of driving it to Reinga and back, and that Joy, a non-mechanical person, would be doing most of the driving. I downloaded the Strava app to keep record and proof of each day's activities.

I purchased a pair of Hoka shoes that were recommended by a Dunedin shoe shop. I planned to get fit on the road. I reasoned, how can you train for 60kms a day, for 40 days without doing 60kms a day? May as well be on the road. I wasn't able to ascertain exactly what the record was for walking the 2100km trip on SH1, but the best I saw was 49 days. So I planned for 40 days with variables. I set up a schedule for the South Island, starting October 17th and a ferry crossing from Picton to Wellington, 19 days later.

I also booked the return crossing for December 3<sup>rd</sup> a month later. I could clearly see the road all the way to Reinga, but couldn't see the trip back. It was out of sight in the future. I had walked 200kms in a single event, but after that I was into the unknown. I planned to research the towns and the townspeople along the way, and keep records of those as I passed. As we live directly on SH1 we had the advantage of leaving home, and then returning four days later. By then we hoped to have a better idea of things we would need. Things a well organised person would have already known about, but which hadn't occurred to me.

I contacted two friends from the running community, to ask for pearls of wisdom. James Harcombe had run round the coastal path of Wales, running around 70kms per day. He had planned well and had a good dedicated support team. He also had a good running buddy in form of Mal Law, who is himself an endurance athlete of some note. James asked about my support team, and was pointedly silent when I said Joy was going to do it. He had met Joy but didn't know her that well, and wondered out loud if she knew what she was in for?

Brooke Thomas, a nurse from Queenstown, had broken the female record for running the Te Araroa Trail, she too had planned well. She had her parents as the main support team. She suggested I not do that, as it's very hard on our nearest and dearest. Both had agreed that the care, prevention, and treatment of blisters was the main issue they encountered on their respective trails. Both also asked if I'd considered how hard, and dangerous, it would be to do this distance on the road? I told them I had. Ha!

## Words from Joy

Rog had indeed talked about walking the length of the country, but it was, in my mind, way off in the future, some other day. How on earth were we suddenly at retirement age and free to do such a thing?

I had finished up the job I had been doing for 12 years as shop/office lady for an engineering firm that serviced the dairy community when Rog retired from Corrections so that we were free to try different things, together. We tried a few weeks of casual orchard work in Ettrick. This was my idea, but I soon decided that it was really hard work, and maybe not my new career. Next, I joined the staff at a local supermarket on a casual contract, and this has fitted in with our periodic wanderings. Food and people are some of my favourite things. My knowledge of plumbing fittings had grown in the engineering job, but if I had had to put together a CV for being the support for a walk up the country in an aged campervan, my relevant skills list would have been a bit lacking.

Driving Licence – Yes. Cooking experience – Some. Mechanical knowledge – Nil.

Navigational skills – A bit average.

Ability to lose track of time while reading a book – THIS is my super power.

Cousins – heeeaps of them – all over the country.

I am really proud to have been part of the Great March North with Rog. I can't say that I enjoyed it all. Some of it was quite stressful, and there was a LOT of time spent parked at the side of the road waiting. I loved improving my geographical knowledge of NZ, and best of all, loved the time with people we connected with on the way. I started writing the 'Things I've learned on the GMN' posts on Facebook and this was a lot of fun, and helped to fill in time – and to process the stressful parts. Humour always helps. Friends – and cousins – responded with fun and encouragement, and it cheered the days. It also got a little addictive.

When we started back down the country after achieving the GMN, I switched to occasional rather than daily updates on the Gentle Saunter South – GSS – to help return to reality.

Enjoy, as you travel with us.


## 3:45pm, October 17th 2021

As I drove Daffy into the carpark at Stirling Point, the famous signpost came into view like the rising sun after a long night. Like the sun it had been there the whole time, it was just my view of it that had been obscured. The signpost itself held aloft important information like how far it is to London, Sydney and New York, and that it was 1401 kms to Cape Reinga (as the albatross glides). It evoked feelings of travel and relative distance.

So many photographs have been taken at this spot, as it's the acknowledged southern end of State Highway 1, if not the southernmost tip of New Zealand, just as Cape Reinga at the other end is not the northernmost tip of the 'Land of the Long White Cloud'. There are vast differences in the reasons pictures are taken by this post. Some are in celebration and represent the culmination of months of hard slog and their eyes are filled with emotion, tears and memory. Some are just to show they were 'here', as they pause for a few moments on their camper tour. These photographers have driven here and will drive away. Some have driven here and will walk away because this spot is the start of the hard slog. I was one of those. I got nervously out of the van and put on my new HOKA shoes. As I jerked the laces tight, I wondered (as I often do at the start of events) how I will feel when I untie them at the end? I'd always loved to walk but I was nervous because I was uncertain whether I could complete the task I had set myself?

I was nervous too because I knew what a stubborn person I am in the face of seemingly impossible odds. These two ingredients cooked together are a recipe for a casserole of suffering. I took a few deep breaths, did some half-hearted stretches, and noticed a few friendly and familiar faces among those standing about. Nicole and Ian, old running buddies, Ian's six-year-old daughter Ella, a woman whose name I couldn't remember and her two dogs. I was a little overwhelmed as I hadn't been expecting anyone.

The dogs were pulling at the lead and whining to go, Nicole's legs were fidgeting with anticipation and Ella was looking at me as if I were Shrek (a goodly monster that her father trusted, but a monster none-the-less) I wasn't sure what Ian had told her about me. Finally he said:

'Did you have a question for Mr Leslie, Ella? Go ahead, he won't bite you!'

She considered this for a moment or two and a variety of emotions flicked across her face, then curiosity and bravery won the day and she decided the risk would be worth it.

'Are you going to walk at night-time as well?'

Ha, good question. I told her I didn't plan to but that sometimes the road can be safer at night. She was satisfied with this response and mightily pleased with her own courage at asking it.

A few obligatory photos were taken at the sign and then at the stroke of 4pm, we were off. I had posted on-line that the pace would be companiable, and companiable it was, even the dogs were happy. Joy drove past us in the camper and the smooth burble of the ancient Rover V8 added to an already congenial atmosphere. I wanted to soak up, not just the history of New Zealand towns on SH1, but who the people were as well, and what had happened in these places. One of the first mail boxes we passed was built into the casing of an outboard motor, speaking of the sea-faring nature of Bluff and its people. Bluff has a relatively long history as far as European settlement is concerned, from the arrival of the first European ship in 1813 (aptly enough named Perseverance) and the beginning of the town some 10 years later.

The Māori had called Bluff Motupohue, 'island of convolvuli. Europeans called it a number of things before settling on Bluff. The first freezing works in Southland was built there over 140 years ago. An Aluminium smelter has been operating over the bay since 1971, and the Foveaux Straight oyster fleet is still based there.

As we left Bluff behind us, we passed the site of the old Ocean Beach Freezing Works which was once the largest meat works in NZ. We were now moving along the newly opened roadside cycle and walking path. Up until only a few weeks previously the words 'Bluff Highway' struck fear into the hearts of all cyclists and walkers who braved it. A hiker I talked to, summed up this way. "I've spent over three months on the TA (Te Araroa) Trail. I've been risking life and limb, crossing flooded mountain streams, climbing snow covered alpine passes, slipping down steep rocky trails, being subjected to extreme weather conditions and stalked by wild dogs, only to find the last 20kms on the Bluff Highway the most terrifying of all. The final link in the trail had just been completed after many years of talk, which as it turned out was a poor substitute for an actual pathway.

New shoes, new path and old friends are a fine combination. The forecast had been for a few showers but the sun shined on our enterprise, with heart-warming benevolence. I had once heard Nicole described as short of leg and mighty in spirit and the 30 kilometres to Invercargill were soon eaten up with the kind of conversation long distance athletes never seem to run out of. She was a police officer and well used to balancing family with work and to the dark under-belly of mental health in our community.

Upon reaching Awarua we decided to leave the trail, which meandered along-side the Waihopai River Estuary, and follow SH1 to Invercargill. It was the first experience of 'walking the road' and this thought made me a bit nervous as I projected my mind forward to the narrow bridges and stretches of highway with little or no verge, that lay waiting over the horizon. This verge was to become my focus for the next forty days. It was dark when we arrived in Invercargill and on the corner of Tay Street and Queen's Drive, we called it a day.

Nicole went off back to her life and my brother-in-law Pete picked me up. We spent a great evening at their place, laughing and sharing fun. The laughter drowned out the nagging concern that I was stiff and foot-sore after only five hours on the road. Tomorrow would be better – 30kms down – only 2070 to go.

# Day 2

## Invercargill to Mataura

There was light rain falling in Invercargill as I set of from the corner of Tay and Queen at 7.00am. This was the beginning of the first real test. Alarmingly I had not managed to slumber away the stiffness in my legs from the short stroll the day before. Pete gave me a farewell hug (he's good at those) and I carried that feeling with me right to Reinga.

Without any fanfare I fixed my eyes on the distant horizon and splashed my way out of town. My feet were wet before I reached the Bill Richard Transport Museum and I looked through the window at some of the old trucks and thought how much better they had weathered the road of life, than I.

The footpath ran out at the Eastern Cemetery and I couldn't help thinking of the battered Mini of 'Goodbye Pork Pie' fame, ending a similar trip at this very spot. I was now confined to the narrow strip along the side of highway one. I was on the verge. On the verge of something great? Or perhaps on the verge of abject failure. This verge would be my intermittent companion and pathway for 37 days. Sometimes it would be wide enough to accommodate two trucks side by side, and sometimes completely non-existent. Southbound trucks would whoosh by with a swirl of misty water buffeting my face and body.

After 3 hours on the hoof I reached the community hall at Dacre and sought shelter there from the southerly wind that was increasingly getting behind the light drizzle. Just along the road my friend David lived with his family and I thought I'd invite myself in for a coffee. As I attempted to call him, I found my hands were almost useless from the creeping cold. As I leaned against the Hall and tried to warm dexterity into my hands, enough to use the phone, a farm dirty utility drove past, slowed, did a U-turn and came back. I had already been offered 2 rides from friendly motorists and had been honing my skills in thanking people with polite refusal. I assumed this was another of those and was distracted by the cold hands phone call.

'Roger Leslie, is that you?' said a familiar voice. 'What the hell are you doing standing on the side of the road in the pouring rain?'

I looked up and there were Tom and Sally* a sharemilking couple I'd known for years. I had met them in another world. As the Area Manager for Corrections Inmate Employment in the newly built Otago Correction Facility, one of my roles had been finding employers brave enough to take on prisoners from the day release programme into their workplaces.

Of course, in the case of farmers, that workplace also included their home and family. This had been seen by many employers as an extremely risky endeavour, but Tom and Sally had offered the chance of a new beginning to many grateful prisoners, and even now years later, many still spoke with emotion of these two and their non- judgmental encouragement. I explained what I was doing and, Tom quipped 'You've always been a bit different.' The issue of mental health was one dear to their hearts, because they had a child with special needs who required almost round the clock care. They had watched their friends raise and enjoy their 'normal' children while they seemed to be on a road that stretched exhaustingly beyond the visible horizon. They seemed happy to talk of their experience and we shared tears and laughter as we recalled people and memories of our connected past.

Reluctantly we finally parted, they to their mud, cows and high needs family and me to the wet road that lay uninvitingly before me. I did though, have a new spring in my step and was glad of the random meeting. Perhaps it wasn't random at all.

A few hundred metres further on I reached the friendly haven of the friends' home and invited myself in for a cuppa. With numb and clumsy fingers I untied my laces and entered another world. A world, wood-burner warm and full of people. They had a tradition that all the adult children who could make it, would come home on a Monday for a family day. There were six daughters with their children and as I wrapped my icy fingers round a hot coffee cup, I was enveloped by warmth of body and spirit. The awkwardness that a stranger always brings to a family situation was soon overrun by friendly banter and the sharing of lives. They were momentarily astounded at my goal and one of the girls spoke for them all when she said:

'I can walk to the mailbox and back, but 2,000kms? I don't think so.' With agile fingers I retied the laces of my soggy shoes, and warm in body and spirit, I set off once more northwards. As I splashed along, I thought of the wonder of families, of how in good times and bad they support each other. They might have their differences but when the rubber hits the road, they are there for each other. As I trudged past the Dacre Radio Antenna and its hundreds of metres of support cables, without which it would fall to the power of wind and weather, I thought of the vast array of signals that fill the air, unheard by human ear.

When one drives a vehicle past this place, normal radio signal is overrun by other band-widths and radio traffic. For a few seconds one is plunged into the world and communications of others before returning to the station to which one had been tuned. I thought of how much a metaphor of life that is.

A green stock truck slowed as it shooshed past and the driver shouted something unintelligible to me which was immediately washed away in the swirling wet. A few kms further on I became aware of the smell of burning rubber in the air, then pieces of shredded tyre started to appear on the road, increasing in size and frequency until finally they lead to the same truck, pulled up unhappily on the verge of the highway with blue smoke rising dramatically from an injured wheel. The driver was standing by it talking on his mobile phone. He gave me wry smile as I passed then finished up his call and called after me:

'Where are you heading mate?' 'Cape Reinga.'

'Cape Reinga?'

'Yep'

'Well you're doing better than me, I'm heading for Temuka and at this rate you'll get there before me. Not long after I gave you shit back there, I blew a tyre and I thought, 'serves you right you dumb bastard" Later as I descended the Edendale Hill the sun came out and with it, Joy in the Camper. She had spent a happy morning with her sister Cheryl in Invercargill and they had chatted and laughed the morning away. Now she was back to the serious business of supporting her slightly nutty husband. She pulled into a side road and I joined her for a late lunch and a small nap. When I awoke, she said:

'While you were sleeping a big green truck tooted to us as he went past, do you know him?'

With new vigour I strolled on and soon passed the Edendale Milk Powder factory which had once been the biggest of its kind in the world. A seemingly endless caravan of tankers came here from all over the South Island. Over the next few weeks I would see most of those tankers and their drivers would greet me enthusiastically and give me as much room as they could as they purred past.

The next factory I passed was the Daiken Particle Board plant near Mataura. Its twin chimneys belched steam into the crisp Southland air, heralding the turning of forest into building material. A steady procession of log trucks was feeding the seeming insatiable appetite for more pine trees. Directly across the river I could see the slopes of Tuturau, located near the east bank of the Mataura River. In 1836 this village had been the scene of the last act of Māori warfare in the South Island.

The sun was setting on my second day as I reached Mataura, but I had to retrace the last kilometre as Joy was having problems with the camper. 'It wouldn't start – it was making a funny noise – stupid camper.' It was like having two friends that don't like each other and you seemed always to be the mediator. It started fine, must have been the rest, and we drove back to Edendale to spend a lovely evening with friends Don and Stephanie.

Fifty kms for the day. Feeling pretty tired and sore. I wondered if I'd be able to keep this up? Then I thought of the stock truck and how invulnerable it looked on the road, but a comparatively small tyre had brought it to a halt. I thought of the road of life, and how others may seem to be unstoppable but we don't know what their journey is really like.

# Day 3

## Mataura to Kuriwao

I got gingerly down from the camper on a cold Mataura morning, somewhat alarmed at the leg stiffness and foot pain. At shoe lace-up I noticed my left foot was swollen and I tried to suppress the niggling fear that this might be the beginning of the end. I had suffered a stress fracture earlier in the year that stubbornly refused to heal and I knew that, like the stock truck, I was most vulnerable where the rubber meets the road. When it came to legs and feet, I could easily be stopped.

You can limp for a kilometre or two but not 2,000. On the positive side the soles were okay and there was no sign of blisters. There was a cold south-westerly blowing, but at least it was coming from behind, so I added that to the blessings, alongside the $2.50 in coins I found in the first 200 metres.

Mataura was in that sleepy stage between the early workers leaving home and the late risers stoking the fires of their bit of the day. I joined a couple of pyjama clad women in Clutterbuck's Supermarket and spent the money on a chocolate bar. There are few things as tasty as a free chocolate bar. The checkout lady asked:

'Where are you heading, all trussed up like that?' 'Cape Reinga.'

'Well good luck with that.'

One of the pyjama maidens offered her opinion: 'F*#% that mate, I can hardly walk across the street!' 'But would you, if you could?'

'Doubt it. Hasn't crossed my mind so far'

On hearing what I was up to, Laura the checkout lady offered to make me a free coffee. The day was looking better and better. I turned onto SH93 to Clinton, which was 8km shorter but hilly. I paused on the middle of the Mataura River bridge and watched the water for a while. The bridge was built in 1939 to replace the many previous efforts to span the gentle river which could at times become a raging torrent, sweeping all before it. The first of these was constructed in 1859 because of the unreliability of the fords. I mused that on this journey I would cross most of NZ's great rivers, and few of the bridges would have walking access like this one. I reflected that many on the journey of mental ill health would be constantly having to overcome obstacles and often without assistance or a safe place to walk.

Looking up the river I tried to imagine the once beautiful Mataura Falls as it had been before the building of a meat works on one side and a paper mill on the other. These two stood with their chimneys jutting arrogantly skyward like two groups of small boys challenging each other across the river and competing to throw the biggest and best stuff into the water. The paper mill dated back to 1876 where although not the first in NZ, was the southern-most in the world and for many years the only one in the South Island.

One of the paper types made here was called Ticket Board which was used for Lotto and TAB tickets, perhaps symbolic of the gamble paper making is. This mill was mothballed some twenty years ago, which is a tragedy in terms of the recycling that went on here, if not for the health of the river. The two factories had been built before the need for much in the way of resource consent and just to show how far we've come, ouvea premix, a by-product dross from the Tiwai Aluminium smelter had been dumped on the site of the paper mill (I use the word dumped, knowing that those responsible would say it was stored, but as no plan to remove it again had been forthcoming, I'll stick with 'dumped').

Ouvea premix gives off toxic ammonia gas when mixed with water so on the banks of Southland's largest river seemed, to them, the best place to 'store' it. For some reason this angered the local inhabitants and the issue even became the subject of a song. ('*Mataura Paper Mill*' by Anthonie Tonnon). Mataura has been home to many famous specimens, producing at least two All Blacks and the great pacer Cardigan Bay. I looked for, and noticed with delight, the riparian planting of native trees and shrubs along the banks of the river. This had been undertaken by local Iwi and had been the success it was, due in most part to the vision and drive of the late great Rewi Anglem, whom I had come to know, like and respect, when he sought help from the two southern prisons to propagate native plants for him. Thanks Rewi!

As I headed out of town, limping on my sore foot, I met the first real hill-challenge of the trek. With the now wet south-westerly blowing fiercely up my well insulated nether parts, I glided smoothly up the slope as if it wasn't there, and best of all the foot was soon forgotten. Perhaps it was pining for some hill work. Joy and the camper swished merrily by and buffeted me with wind and wet, but I was in a good place and my world, although small, was a happy one. This route, also known as the Old Coach Road, was that day also the Old Walker Road.

The camper was sitting like a safe harbour in a storm, at the site of an old sod cottage which had been built here in 1857 as a stage station serving the Dunedin-Invercargill inland coach route. As I read the plaque, I wondered about the tough people who braved this road in the 1870s, knowing that they may have to wait on the water to go down at the Mataura ford before crossing. I wondered what they would think of me and my quest. I climbed thankfully into the warm haven of the camper, where a pot of water was boiling away merrily on the gas stove. I heard a far-away disembodied voice calling my name and as I couldn't see Joy, I wondered if I was colder than I realised. The muted voice persisted and I finally tracked it down to the toilet cubical. Joy had locked herself in there and was starting to panic about the pot on the stove. The toilet door did not always co-operate when the camper was not parked on the flat. She was a bit snooty about the whole thing but busied herself with warming her silly old husband up. I gratefully wrapped my gloved fingers round a lovely cup of coffee and breathed the great Scottish aroma of porridge.

I don't normally eat porridge at 10am but there was little that was normal about this juncture in my life. The porridge heated me from the inside out, and man, did I need it. I was well clothed with several layers of insulation, but the persistent cold had soaked into my back and chest, leaving me deeply chilled. While we were resting there, a passing truck greeted us with a prolonged blast of the airhorn. It was a bulk cement truck and would be our old friend James from Otakia. He is a dairy farmer who moonlighted occasionally as a truck driver. Coffee, porridge, warmth, girlfriend and a companionable toot from James, all went together to lift my chilled spirits.

Setting off again I climbed the Otaraia Pass and descended into the Otago watershed. As I passed the Otago sign, the sun came out, and with it a creeping warm that infused my bones. I came at last to the sign pointing to Owaka where Joy and I had both grown up. We had lived there, raised our children there, buried a daughter there, cried there and laughed there. In Owaka (the place of the canoe) we had learned to be us. We had learned to paddle our canoe and in the calm waters and rough rapids, to have empathy for those whose lives hadn't followed fairy tale storylines. We had lived there until I had 'done the prison thing'.

I met SH1 again at Clinton, which is 'more than a one-horse town', no really it is, there are five. I had a Jimmy's Pie there because I was as close to Roxburgh, the home of Jimmy's Pies, as I would get, and headed for Kuriwao. I wondered about going further but my feet said "No!" so I lay in the tall grass, looking up into the clear blue sky, and waited for Joy to finish the chapter in her book. We drove to Amy's place. Amy is a niece of Joy's, who with her husband Hamish, farms in the Kuriwao area. She had known of the planned walk to Reinga but had perhaps not processed the reality until confronted with the semi- crippled old man sitting in her lounge. She was no coward and voiced what most were thinking.

'You're nuts Uncle Rog!'

Day three was over – 56 kms and 527 metres of elevation.

*Joy Leslie: Things learned on the Great March North:*

1. *Always duck your head when moving from the back to the front of the camper.*
2. *Never completely shut the door of the toilet, when in camper alone.*

# Day 4

## Kuriwao to Milburn

As I laced up my shoes for the fourth leg, I noted that my left foot was still swollen but thankfully not painful. I hoped this was a good sign (us road walkers are big on signs). One unwelcome sign was a sore throat, which I hoped wouldn't, as a result of bitterly cold weather over the last days, turn into a heavy cold. Happily full of a hearty farm breakfast, eaten in the familiar turmoil of kids getting ready for school, I set off into the sunrise. This was my first experience of the rising sun as it had been wet the two previous mornings.

I had an appointment to talk to a classroom full of children at Rosebank Primary School in Balclutha at 10.00am. This meant 21 kilometres in three hours so I needed to lift the average speed to 7kph. I had been holding myself to 6kph, hoping that happy medium could be maintained for the whole journey. A road safety problem arose with the morning sun. When I had to cross to the left side for corners etc., I had to be aware that following traffic had difficulty discerning me against the brightness of the sun, and my fluorescent clothing was almost useless.

I walked off into the gravel, and sometimes the grass, as I heard vehicles bearing down on me from behind. It was amazing how much my hearing had become my most acute sense. I could discern from other traffic noise, whether vehicles were coming or going, if they were slowing or accelerating, and even if they were light or heavy traffic. Occasionally I'd hear the brrap, brrap, brrap, of heavy tyres crossing the centre medium as good truck drivers moved over to give me a safe margin. I always acknowledged such professionalism with a wave.

I was now well and truly into South Otago and walked past many fields I had ploughed years ago as an agriculture contractor in the area. One such paddock was etched in my memory as I had ploughed it through the dark hours of a rainy night. The terrain was relatively steep and while wet turf is easily turned by a plough, traction is harder to come by. With a reversible plough, one normally doesn't need to drive on the turned furrows, but this was no normal paddock. Because of the steepness of the slope I had driven onto the furrows to turn the tractor round, and the plough over. Suddenly the wet furrows underneath the tractor started sliding and the whole turnout went sideways into the gully. Obviously, I'd survived this, but it had been a bad, few moments. I could still picture it, and smell the wet soil and fear. As the powerful lights pointlessly illuminated the driving rain fore and aft, we slid sideways into the dark abyss. When everything came to an uncertain halt, I sat for some time breathing deeply, and trying to relax the death grip I had on the steering wheel. That was from another chapter in my life, so I could now just smile and walk away. It hadn't been quite that simple all those years ago.

I marched purposely down into Balclutha with time in hand and arrived at the school as the kids were going out for a break. We had a light morning tea with the teachers and discussed my activities and plans with them. The classrooms of our two grandchildren, Eliza and Zeke were to be joined for my presentation. They were very proud of having their Opa and Nana to show off to class-mates.

I sat among a sea of red tee-shirts, and like the sea, they were constantly moving, rustling and lapping over my feet. They were a bit young for deep insights into mental health but they did know that excessive screen time, especially at night, would be bad for the mind. When I asked for questions, the most pressing need for information was:

'Why have you got a sticky on your leg?

'Because sometimes, I don't look where I'm going and I fall down the bank.'

'What's that tube sticking out of your pack?'

'It's my drinking tube.'

'Where's the drink?'

'Let me show you the bladder.' 'Can we touch it?'

'Go ahead!'

All the questions were asked in the correct school manner, with raised hands and polite waiting. Zeke, who was 7, had his hand up and was earnestly waiting his turn. When I asked him what his question was, he smiled and said 'I forgot.' Just didn't want to miss out. None of us do.

The teachers thanked us profusely for the visit, saying they didn't get visits like that anymore, and that the mental health of children was one of un-talked about negatives of lockdowns.

I headed through town, across the Clutha River and out into the hills, where a sign informed me about 'wind gusts.' Those drivers that have had their trucks flipped on their sides there, would probably dispute whether the word 'gusts' really cuts the mustard as sufficient warning. A little further along another ambiguous sign caught my attention, 'Old Sod Cottage' seemed a bit restrictive.

Soon I was faced with the most dangerous bridge thus far on SH1 (for foot traffic), where it crosses the main trunk railway line at Crichton. The bridge is humped and curved and has a blind corner at the North end. I stood for a long time waiting until I could hear no traffic and had plucked up the courage to make a walk for it. In the end the courage came, but then so did the traffic. I thought of how rivers and roads are a lot like life, when the course is straight and wide, we are never really tested, but when a narrow corner, bridge or gorge comes along, the pressure really comes on.

With that behind me, the road opened up to the Moneymore Plains and Milton, which boasted itself as the 'Town of Opportunities'. The Woollen Mill, that had once been the main employer of the town, had been long since closed and the main employer is now the Corrections Department in the new prison along the road. A sad reflection of the 'progress' we've made. There were bright spots of local firms bucking the trend of disintegration, like McLay Boats and Calder Stewart, who were refusing to accept the stereotype and still challenging the big boys in bigger towns.

The day was well spent when I reached Milburn and walked past the Otago Corrections Facility, known locally as the 'Milton Hilton'. We drove to friends Stafford and Melissa, where I had a blissful soak in their spa. Fifty-five kms and 550 metres of climbing was a good day, if only I didn't hurt so much.

**Joy Leslie: Things learned on the Great March North:**

3.   *Always turn the lights off when parked, to avoid having to use the jumper cables to restart the camper.*

# Day 5

## Milburn to Dunedin

As I laced up my shoes in Milburn, a prison van rumbled by, transporting prisoners to the Dunedin Court. I wondered how the day would end for those guys? Some would be released, some would be bailed, and some would be returned to the negative world that is prison, where in my view, only lip-service would be paid to their mental health needs and none to that of their families.

I was planning to sleep in my own bed that night and I set off, glad to be free, glad the swelling had gone in my foot, and glad the expected exhaustion had not overwhelmed me on day 4. This was a piece of road I had walked, cycled and driven many times over the years I had worked in the prison, and I was happily familiar with it. Lake Waihola loomed up, heralded by the sign 'No doctor, no hospital, one cemetery', which seemed quite appropriate, given the number of fatal accidents signalled by crosses on the roadside. I stopped for a cuppa with my good friend and brother-in-law Alf. He asked:

'How long will it take you to do the walk?'

'Elijah, in the Bible, walked for 40 days, so I'm sort of basing my expectations on that.'

'Elijah was fed by an angel.'

'I have been too.'

I, bypassing the flood free highway and its narrow bridges, took instead the old main road through Titri and Henley. The ancient single-lane bridge over the Taieri River brought back plank rattling memories of sitting there in the family car, waiting for our turn to cross. I met Josh along the road, a young farmer friend, and he stopped his mule for a chat. He is a perpetual smiler and his demeanour exuded enthusiasm which filled my tired old body with the inkling that I might just make it. I wished I could have taken him with me. He seemed to think my success was a foregone conclusion.

This was a day for encouragement because as I put Allanton behind me, I was assailed by the happy blast of car horn, and there was Chander Harjinder Singh (Harry, for short), a well-known and loved lunatic of Dunedin's ultra-running scene. Harji had run marathons in gumboots and overalls and broken the record of ascents of Baldwin Street (the World's steepest) to raise awareness of the plight of his farming colleagues in India. He walked with me a for while then, to the sound of gloomping wellies, he sprinted back to his car and was off. A few more kilometres along the way, I came to an intersection where a friend had been knocked off his bike and killed. He had been my high-school maths teacher and had reached through the fogs of learning difficulty in my brain in a way very few teachers had. He had taken me under his wing and taught me a lot of things besides maths and science. I stood and thought about him, eyes hot with unshed tears, until I needed to do something, so I sent a text to his widow. Then I felt much better and set off again, rejuvenated. Half an hour later I reached our home, I lived on SH1 and this wee walk was just checking out the street from end to end. It had taken 2.5 hours to drive to Bluff and 4 days to walk back. Jamie and Aileen were waiting there to join us and add their considerable event organising talents to our enterprise. They had for many years organised the Great Naseby Water Race and were no strangers to suffering and broken athletes. In that race you could choose your brand of endurance from 50kms to 200kms, and now, even 200 miles. Jamie himself had completed a number of milers (160kms) and even though he's a runner, he had condescended to walk with me to Waikouaiti, some 60kms away.

With a good cup of home-brewed coffee and a few of Joy's fantastic muffins under the belt, we were off again, leaving the girls to natter about how stupid their husbands were. Jamie and I had plenty of catching up to do and the kilometres quickly melted away. As we descended into Fairfield we met John, a gnarly old bike rider from the Taieri who had, among other things, competed in the TA Bike event, riding from Reinga to Bluff through some of NZ's wildest country. He didn't want to hold us up so rode along with us as we walked and talked of ultra-events and eventers. My aches and pains were momentarily forgotten.

As we went over Lookout Point and descended into Dunedin, I smelt the sea for the first time since leaving Bluff. I wondered how I would feel, when (or if) I finally smelled it at Reinga. The distant cape was looking and feeling further away each step I took. We walked past the Cadbury Chocolate Factory that had been an icon in Dunedin for over a hundred years but had been closed in the interests of profit. The new hospital would be built on this site, maybe. We pulled the pin by the Botanical Gardens in North Dunedin and, after poorly communicating where we were, had to retrace the last 1,000 steps. It seemed an awfully long way back.

As I went to save the day's walk on the Strava app, I noticed it had recorded 68.4kms. I knew that wasn't right and on investigation discovered the recording had started at last night's accommodation and not at Milburn, thus adding 12kms to the total. Still, 56.4kms wasn't too bad, and was, up until then the best day. If only I hadn't felt so tired.

As I had anticipated, sleeping in my own bed was fantastic. I wouldn't be back there for two months.

# Day 6

## Dunedin to Waikouaiti

Lacing up my shoes for Day Six required the use of the coffee table as I couldn't bend down far enough for this simple task. Everything hurt, even my shoulders and neck. The sore throat I'd had the day before was now a head cold with a developing cough. Just what I needed. We packed the camper with six weeks in mind rather than four days, and tried to think of everything we might need for the massive task ahead. Joy gave final instructions to our boarder about her house plants, and we were off, into the unknown. We drove back to the Botanical Gardens where we had finished day five and met up with Jamie and Aileen. Jamie observed that 'I looked like shit' – we have that kind of relationship – here in the southern ultra-running world that kind of thing is encouragement of the highest order. Aileen said:

'Go on, you mad buggers, get out of here!'

So off we went along North East Valley, taking the first of many detours to avoid motorways. I texted my daughter Miriam, who lives in the valley that we would be passing by if she cared to join us. She replied an hour later when we were well on our way up Mount Cargill Rd, asking:

'Where are you?'

She had underestimated, not for the first time, how fast I walk, and missed us. She hopped in her car and overtook us at the top of the hill. It was time for a break anyway. She wondered out loud if she would see me again (alive) and gave me a farewell hug. This walking long distances, makes one quite thin-skinned in more than just the feet and I may have let a wee tear slip through.

As we left Dunedin behind and wound our way down into Waitati, we met Sally, an old running friend who was trotting (as one does) the 20kms to Dunedin to pick up her car from the garage. Old running friend, as in, the relationship was old, not Sally. She is one of the toughest people I've ever met and well wishes from her were in strong currency. She said:

'There's some roadworks back there, but if you're nice to them they'll let you through.'

And so it turned out. We stood obediently by the 'Stop' sign and chatted with the lollypop man until we got the green light to go. He spoke into his radio as we left:

'There's some more nut jobs coming through, heading for Cape Reinga, this lot. No, I kid you not.'

It seemed this was not an 'every day' occurrence. The second lollypop man was surprised to see us, believing he was being 'had on.' He asked:

'Are you really walking to Cape Reinga?'

To which Jamie replied, 'This old codger is?'

Waitati – formerly known as Waitete – is a little town on the shores of Blueskin Bay which was famous in the 1960s for its hippies and it seemed that many of them had never left. The Waitati Militia was formed then, complete with uniforms and canon, as a protest against the Vietnam War. The Militia is still going strong and so is the flower power feel to Waitati. The area had been named 'Blueskin' by early whalers and was believed to be in reference to a heavily tattooed Ngāi Tahu chief.

Aileen had used her eventing skills to arrange free coffees and muesli bars at the Blueskin Gallery, so we sat down and soaked up the aroma of kindness. SH1 was just across the road and the sound of heavy traffic finally brought us back to the task on hand. For the next 30 days, pleasures could be had, but always with underlying guilt of brevity and the gathering cloud of continued pain. Having joined SH1 again, we headed along to the bottom of the Kilmog and took the scenic route via the coast road to Karitāne. On this stretch we came to the site of the Seacliff Mental Hospital which has such a damming history in the treatment of mental illness. It was once called a Lunatic Asylum. No doubt, good things were done there but it is mostly remembered for the bad. It was opened in 1884, and had over 500 inmates at its peak. The main building was closed in 1958. In 1942, one of New Zealand's worst fire disasters occurred, when 37 out of 39 patients in the locked Ward Five of Seacliff hospital died. For periods between 1947 and 1955 Janet Frame, one of New Zealand's most accomplished writers, was a patient at Seacliff. She had been mistakenly diagnosed as schizophrenic.

It was hard to shake the memory of Seacliff from my mind as we walked on, but Jamie is a good companion and as we descended into Karitāne I remembered a better part of the tortured history of this coastline. Karitāne had given its name to nurses who were trained to work with mothers and newborn babies under Truby King's scheme. Sir Truby was the first superintendent of the Seacliff Hospital and had set up this training hospital in Karitāne.

Soon we were back out on SH1 again and closing in on Waikouaiti, where we planned to call it a day. Crossing the Waikouaiti River involved another narrow and dangerous bridge but we made it across alive. We stopped and posed for a photo in front of a Second-Hand shop in town which was appropriately called 'The Oddity'.

We went 'down to the sea again, to the lonely sea and the sky' and soaked our unhappy feet in the freezing water. While the fire in my feet was replaced by cold numbness, I had a hot spot on my left heel that I hoped was only a passing thing.

It wasn't.

We sadly said goodbye to Jamie and Aileen and spent the evening with Peter and Thelma, some other friends just a few hundred metres back from the beach, where we yarned and laughed well into the night. 45kms for the day but more importantly, 800 metres of vertical, which would turn out to be the most for a single day in the South Island.

# Day 7

## Waikouaiti to Maheno

By the time I laced up my shoes on Day Seven, I was already well acquainted with my new blister. She had awoken me several times in the night, wanting constant attention. In the cold light of dawn she turned out to be a grape sized appendage under my left heel callous, a deep tissue blister. I tried to convince myself it would be okay once I was on the move and everything had warmed up, but I couldn't get rid of the dark cloud developing on the horizon of my mind.

I'd had blisters before and got over them, but I'd never done this while walking 10 or more hours each day on the unyielding surface of a road. James and Brooke had both warned me 'Watch out for the blisters!' I dressed her in the finest that money could buy, and shut her into the shoe. My sore throat of the last two days had now developed into a good old country head cold. We had a happy breakfast with Peter and Thelma and I borrowed a book I saw on their shelf, 'The Bielski Brothers' by Peter Duffy, I thought I may as well keep my spirits up by reading of someone else who had overcome adversity.

We drove back to The Oddity shop and I got gingerly out of the camper. No more hopping out, springing out, or any other 'out' that didn't involve great care. In fact there would be no more of that short of Reinga. There was instant protest from my body, a full march of protesters with coloured banners, chanting and even a megaphone. My body had no way of knowing this was a multi-day event having never experienced such a thing. My brain alone knew the plan, and callously dismissed the protest by turning on the lawn sprinklers. I limped off down the main street of Waikouaiti and out of town into the unknown. Agatha, I had decided to name my blisters, had the megaphone and kept ranting long after the others had put road cones over the sprinklers and retired to wait this out. I tried hard not to limp, knowing the collateral damage this does, but pain is a powerful influencer. My mind was running things and seemed to be the only strong one that morning. I wondered though, how long that would be enough to keep the show on the road?

Not far out of town I came across Goodwood where, before some serious road re-alignment had been done, there had been a dangerous curve called 'the Goodwood Corner'. Here, while volunteering for St John Ambulance in Dunedin, I'd attended the worst road traffic accident I would ever see. A young teenage girl had been roused from her bed in the early hours of the morning to be the sober driver for some friends and drive them home. They had done everything right, but this car-load of teenage promise had been smashed to a heap of pitiful debris by a drunk driver coming the other way. The four crosses on the bank, stood in silent testimony to that night. I got used to it, but I never got over it, and the whole thing overwhelmed me again.

In the distance I could see the cone shape of Puketapu and knew that meant Palmerston wasn't too far off. Puketapu (sacred hill) is a 393-metre hill that watches over the township, and is where an annual race is held called Kelly's Canter. During WW2 local Police Constable Bert Kelly had jogged (in uniform) to the top of the hill to check for enemy shipping and other signs of invasion. The race to commemorate that has been held over 50 times, with PC Kelly himself starting the runners off for the first few years. Most Otago runners and the odd walker (some very odd) have done this event.

Palmerston is also where SH85, otherwise known as the 'Pigroot', begins and gives access to the Maniototo. I wasn't sure of the origin of the pigroot title but I recalled a senior ambulance officer once driving his car determinedly into one of these animals while speeding to a call.

The pig won the day, and left the scene of the accident under its own steam, the car didn't.

While I was using the public toilet, there was a commotion outside and the raised voices of a small boy and his grandmother. He apparently didn't want to go to the toilet but she was insisting. Finally he came in, but didn't use the toilet, then refused to leave. She was forced to enter herself, apologising profusely to the blokes present, and take matters (and the boy) into her own hands. It isn't all beer and skittles being a grandparent.

I had considered taking a detour from Palmerston through Trotters Gorge to Moeraki but Agatha was still in full voice so I stayed with SH1 where the hills were less and the road smoother. I was glad of this decision when I reached Shag Point because I was able to walk along Katiki Beach. The protesters were unhappy about the scramble down onto the beach, but the sound of their voices was soon drowned out by sound of the sea. This would turn out to be the only walk on a beach for the whole journey. Joy parked at the far end and came back to meet me. Walking hand-in-hand along the beach was the highlight of the day. There was no traffic, no hard asphalt, no narrow bridges, and for a time, not a peep from Agatha. The spell was broken when I re- joined SH1 and was immediately confronted with an overhead bridge crossing the main trunk railway line. It seemed railway bridges were the narrowest of them all and this one was no exception. I selected a reasonable gap in the heavy traffic and scampered to safety. Agatha was against that too, but she was overruled by popular vote.

I walked past Moeraki, with its famous spherical boulders and only a fleeting desire to visit the beach itself. The idea of clambering up onto a boulder with my feet the way they were was not a happy picture. Hampden was not far away and we had been invited for a cuppa with Donna, who had lived near us on the Taieri and had moved to this picturesque wee coastal town. She was fascinated with my walk and made me promise to come and talk to the Oamaru Tramping Club when I was finished. She seemed to have no doubt at all that I could, and more importantly would, do it. I mentioned this to my feet when I was back on the road, but they were unimpressed and just grumbled. I stopped to read the history of the Waianakarua Mill house which had been built in 1879 of locally quarried stone blocks, and operated as a flour mill until 1939. The historic bridge over the river is still there to be seen. I had driven past this spot hundreds of times but had never stopped to actually look. This was now becoming the theme of my walk. Stopping to look, and consider.

The last 10kms from Hebert to Maheno were lost in the blur of mind- over-matter. The only thing I recall clearly, is chuckling as I passed Happy Valley Rd. Nobody was happy in my valley. My head cold was here for the long haul. Joy was waiting with the camper at the Gull Service Station in Maheno, where the fuel price was the lowest we were to see for the whole trip. We drove the camper across the road, and parked at the Maheno Country Tavern. For a gold coin donation they had lovely showers.

One bright spot on the thunder clouded horizon. I had walked 62.5kms – the best day yet.

# Day 8

## Maheno to Waimate

As I laced up for Day Eight, I was in a sorry state. I'd slept hardly at all. I had a full-blown cold. I was congested, coughing and unhappy. Agatha had swollen grotesquely and I had to relieve the pressure again before re-dressing the entire foot. I now had hot-spots on both sides of my right heel as well. I ate my porridge with a heavy sense of dread. I tip-toed out onto the road, not in the sense of being quiet, but because I couldn't bear any weight on my heels. I stood there on the side of the road and thought about doing the sensible thing and going back to bed. But I didn't. I put my stubborn old head down and set off resolutely for Oamaru, 13kms away, where I planned to meet Joy, and together attend a church service. Crossing the Kakanui River, I knew I had reached the beginning of the Totara Estate which, in 1866 was purchased by the NZ & Australian Land Co and boasted 15,000 acres, 17,600 sheep and 200 cattle. One of the parts of the Estate was the flour mill across the river from Maheno, known as Clark's Mill, which is an operating museum, and was one of the 13 mills in North Otago. It took me more than an hour to walk from one end of the old Estate to the other. From here 1882 the first shipment of NZ frozen mutton was transported to England, a journey that took some three months. As I walked along, I thought of William Davidson, the manager of the Estate at the time who believed it could be done, but had to ignore all expert advice of the naysayers. He backed himself and just went ahead and accomplished something that would, in the end, earn the country more than any other single export. Thinking about this almost made me forget my woes, and the state of my feet. Almost.

I arrived in downtown Oamaru around 9.00am, and Joy turned up too, right on time. The camper though, was a sorry sight. It was streaming water from every orifice like Godzilla freshly risen from the sea. Joy had forgotten to leave the hot tap open while travelling (as per instructions in the manual) and had blown a water pipe. Things were terse between us. She was apologetic, and I was making a poor effort of keeping a lid on my emotions, which were already worn thin by my physical condition. Here in the Steampunk Capital of New Zealand, I had no outlet for my own steam. I was exasperated but desperately wanted to keep her on the team. I needed her. Then into the middle of all this, stepped Brooke, the TA Trail record-holder herself, and gave me a supportive hug. The timing was impeccable, if ever I'd needed encouragement, it was then. She and her friend Adam were on their way to Nelson and keeping an eye out for us. They had been following my Fb posts and knew we were in this area somewhere.

Brooke brimmed with freshness, fitness and exuberance, and some of this soaked into me, sweeping away the spirit of moroseness, that was threatening to drive me into the ground. Brooke stayed to help Joy dry up the innards of the camper and Adam walked with me through Oamaru to Orana Park. He is a personal trainer in the field of ultra-marathons and he cunningly lifted my eyes back to the goal on hand and made me believe again. He has a collection of photos on his website of extreme athletes in, what he calls, the 'hurt locker' and I suspect there's one of me in there too. He reminded me that he had been present when I had completed the 200km race at Naseby, and he wanted to see that look on my face again. Suffice to say, the passing encouragement from Brooke and Adam lifted me out of the 'sloth of despond' and put wind again in my sails.

My feet still hurt and I still had a cold, but I was infused with unquenchable positivity. Brooke and Adam drove away and we two went to church around the corner, which was similarly uplifting. There's nothing like a good hearty bit of singing to bring perspective to one's pathway.

It was a different Roger that got back on the road after lunch, and headed north, past the racecourse out of town. Soon I reached the Pukeuri Corner, where SH83 heads off towards the mountains. I love the mountains, and would normally much sooner have gone there, but my mountains on this trip were different. They weren't snow-capped or particularly high, but the mountains of the mind, and its relationship with the body. They were more like the Eiger, which can be ascended by train, or by the slightly more difficult route up the North Face, which has taken many lives and few prisoners.

The Pukeuri Meat Works stood there at the junction, as it had for over 100 years, and has been a major source of employment in Oamaru for all this time. A few kilometres further I came to a plaque informing me I was standing on the 45th Parallel and that it was the same distance to both the Equator and South Pole. Good to know these things.

The hills of Otago were now behind me and there wouldn't be any more until well past Christchurch. Now it was the plains with straight roads and faster traffic. I hadn't been looking forward to this part but I found I was adapting to each piece of road as I came to it. Now I had to be more aware of traffic sound. It amazed me how the mind could separate the different sounds from the constant noise. Vehicles that were coming towards me, vehicles that were heading away, light traffic, heavy traffic, and vehicles that were drifting over the rumble strip, and therefore into my safety zone. One example of this latter group, looked up from her lap, where I assume she was keeping track of her social media profile, as she was about to skittle me, and swerved violently back into the middle of the road. Still imprinted on my memory, is the look of shocked surprise on her face, tinged with a little guilt. A burst of adrenaline fizzed through my veins and I gave vent to an involuntary commentary on her driving. Afterwards though, the post adrenaline low was so bad, I had to sit down for a wee regroup. It had been a very close thing.

After a time the trembling in my legs dissipated and I was off again, but walking a lot closer to the grass. As I neared the Waitaki Bridge,

I found Joy parked in a small layby, and stopped for a welcome break. Also stopped there were Richard and Dianne, some friends from our home-town and we enjoyed a leisurely hour of supportive banter. Kiwi culture, particularly rural Kiwi culture dictates that, in a close and therefore safe friendship, any support is hidden deep within a critical summary of one's recent activities. They seemed to be of the view that Joy deserved a lot of sympathy for supporting her husband in his time of madness. The rules of engagement in these exchanges, are that the women will side with each other with the blokes taking the opposing view, but I seemed to be on my own this time. The case for the defence was weak enough with my crippled feet and heavy cold, so I didn't bother to share of the recent altercation with the car.

The Waitaki River Bridge, all 914 metres of it, had been weighing on my mind. This is not the sort of distance one can await a gap in the traffic flow, then 'scamper' across. I had driven across hundreds of times and as a family game, we used to see who could hold their breath all the way across, but I had never viewed it through the eyes of a walker. It was with some relief that as I approached, I found a concrete abutment some 600mm wide between the railing and carriageway. I was able to walk from Otago to Canterbury in relative safety, if not immunity. As I walked, I started to relax (a bit) and noticed the remnants of other times and other bridges that had spanned the wide braided river. I had taken the time to research this river crossing, and knew that in 1876 a bridge catering for both road and rail was opened, and that this had remained until 1956 when the current structure was opened for road traffic only. Indeed the old bridge had been crossed in 1954 by the Royal Train carrying the new Queen Elizabeth on her tour of the realm. Sadly the new arrangement did not cater for horse or foot traffic. All in the name of progress, as this had long been an issue. An article in the *Timaru Herald* (1877) referred to river drownings as the 'New Zealand Disease'.

The walk from the river to Waimate was as unremarkable as the countryside. I had shut my mind down to anything other than survival.

My goal of 60kms for the day would end at Waimate, and I watched for the brightly painted yellow shed with the hopping wallaby, that would signify that milestone. I was in Canterbury. In spite of the hold-ups I had still covered 60kms. Over the last eight days I had walked 415kms and climbed 3385 vertical metres. My body was a physical wreck, but my mind was blinking away the tears of doubt, and focusing on Reinga. It was just up the road. A bit.

*Joy Leslie: **Things learned on the Great March North:***

4. *ALWAYS turn off the water pump and leave the hot tap open before driving the camper.*
5. *Sitting with the door and windows open helps to dry the camper out.*
6. *On a more positive note, I also learned this morning that I still have enough volume when singing in church to make someone in front of me turn around for a look.*

# Day 9

## Waimate to Temuka

Lace-up on Day Nine was a long and painful business. After a mostly sleepless night, getting down from the over-cab bed took a long time. The foot inspection part of the day was depressing to say the least. Sort of like inspecting the troops at Dunkirk. 'Let's get out of here as best we can, and live to fight another day.' I had a new and serious deep tissue blister on my right heel. This one I named Rosette. Agatha and Rosette (Agro for short) both needed pressure released just to get them into my shoes. I packed some hiker's wool around them, and eased the socks into place.

The socks were proper padded racing socks designed for specific feet, but in my munted state of body and mind I put them on the wrong feet. I didn't care. I wasn't going to go through that business again. My feet seemed so far away, or maybe my arms were shrinking. Eating the now standard bowl of porridge filled me with primeval courage, as it no doubt had my ancestors, years ago in the Highlands of Scotland. I wondered if they would have been proud of me.

I would have liked a skirl of pipes to set me on my way, but this would probably not have gone down well with the other inhabitants of the Camper Park, so I left in silence. The warm-up stage of the day's walk took much longer than usual and I was glad to stop and read some history as I passed through the town. There was a massive mural painted on the side of some grain hoppers behind Waimate Transport.

It depicted Michael Studholme, an early settler, greeting Te Huruhuru a local Māori Chief with a hongi. In 1854 Studholme had purchased the land that would become the Te Waimate sheep run, and these two men had reached an intercultural understanding that few had managed at the time, and with which the country was still struggling.

Because I knew it was there, I sought out, in Seddon Square, the memorial statue of Margaret Cruickshank a local doctor who had lived, worked and died here in Waimate during the 1918 Flu Epidemic. She was one of 14 doctors throughout the country to die. The terrible twins, Agatha and Rosette were having a contest to see which could scream the loudest but their squabbling was reduced to murmur as I read the history of this fantastic woman. Margaret and her twin Christina were born down the road in Palmerston in 1873. Their mother had died when they were just ten, so they attended the District High School on alternate days while the other looked after the five younger children.

In the evenings the twin that had been to school, would relate to the other what she had learned. They were co-duxes of Otago Girl's High School and both went on to University study. Margaret became the first registered female doctor in New Zealand when she started work in Waimate. When her practice partner went off for active duty in 1914, she carried the burden alone. When the Flu Epidemic struck in 1918, she worked tirelessly to care for stricken patients. One poignant memory of her, was when an entire household was struck down, she milked their cow so they would have some sustenance. She was struck down herself in November of that year and died, being just 45. The business of my blisters was forced to take a back seat in the presence of these great people, and I headed out of town, with my head full of important pioneers.

I re-joined SH1 at Wainono Junction and set off for Makikihi. Along the way I was enthralled by fields of rapeseed in full bloom on both sides of the road. Joy was waiting in Makikihi, a town made famous by the potato chip, which is a staple of New Zealand diet. The day was turning into a hot one and I needed a lot of fluid to keep hydrated. The problem with ignoring signals from my feet and body was that I tended not to listen to any of the signals. Each day Joy was more and more taking over the decision making of what I would eat and when. She was waiting again in St Andrews where SH1 meets the sea again.

St Andrews reminded me of my father, who had a strange fetish about the little town. He would take what he called a 'short cut' by driving down a back street (there is only one) to 'miss out the built-up area'. It was a nonsense, because the distance was the same and required three sharp right angle turns instead of one. In memory of him I took the 'short cut'. It made me smile, and smiles were highly valuable on my journey. Dad had worked in the Waimate area when he was young, indeed he was there when he met my mother who was nursing in Oamaru. Once he brought the family up to visit his old boss, and during a bit of free time, my brother and I had thrown an experimental stone at a magpie. Obviously only one of us had thrown the stone, but I can't remember which one, so I only bring him into the tale to share the burden of blame. To our great surprise, and no doubt to that of the bird, we scored a direct hit and it fell 'stone dead' to the ground. We buried the evidence and didn't report the crime until some time later, when dad was in a good mood. He just smiled wryly and said,

'They're a pack of blighters anyway, so don't worry about it!'

In the 1960s the Australian magpie was not found any further south than the Waitaki River. Now they are busy causing damage to native bird species all over NZ. As I walked out of St Andrews, every time I saw a magpie, I knew we'd done our bit to slow down the spread.

As I was crossing the Pareora River bridge, I saw two $2 coins on the road and took my life in my hands in scooping them up. There was a dairy at the turn-off to the freezing works and there I purchased an ice-cream. When you are hot and tired, an ice-cream purchased with free money tastes better than anything imaginable.

Miriam, an old friend, had promised to meet me and do the walk into Timaru. She had shared many extreme events with me over the years, like the Old Ghost Ultra, the WUU2K, the Molesworth Challenge, and the Big Easy. The year I competed in the 200kms at

Naseby, she had been there too, doing the 'cruisy' 100kms which she went on to win. She had started at 6am on the Saturday, when I had already been going for 22hrs. I was pretty tired and just when I needed that pre- dawn mental boost the way one always does in all-night races, Miriam came trotting along, and provided it. Her industrial sized head-lamp lighting up the water-race track like day, and drowning my pathetic little pool of light into insignificance. She slowed down walked with me a little way to encourage me, then trotted easily off on her long fit looking legs. I saw those same long, fit looking legs get out of a car which had pulled up at Kingsdown. It was Miriam being dropped off by her husband Dave. He is also a 'bit of a runner' and no stranger to ultra events in the mountains. He is also 'one of the Bielski Brothers'. Miriam and I had much to catch up on, and the kilometres into Timaru just melted away. She came from Ireland and I'm such a sucker for an Irish accent. As we meandered along the footpaths of town, another car pulled up and an athletic bloke hopped out, laced on his running shoes, abandoned his wife and kids, and joined us. He called to his wife:

'When you've finished the shopping, text me and I'll tell you where we are.' She had that same look on her face that my wife has when I say:

'Didn't I tell you? I've got a race on this Saturday!'

This was Steve another ultra stalwart, and three of us were off again. Joy had gone to her cousin Julie's house in Hassall St, and we dropped in there for a cuppa and a short break. Because I had reinforcements from the ultra-world, there wasn't the same questioning about my sanity. I dared not stay too long because Julie's garden was quite the botanical siren, that could easily have lured one onto the rocks of indolence. Setting off again, I was amazed at how much easier it was to ignore the protest of body and feet, when among friends.

Steve's family caught up on us at Washdyke, faces shining with post-shopping exuberance, and he reluctantly returned to his other life. I had been telling him of the dark place I had been in mentally and physically, only the day before, and rather than being appalled, his eyes had glowed with envy and FOMO (fear of missing out). I think he was seriously considering throwing his life away and coming with me.

The last 15kms to Temuka seemed such a piece of cake, when compared to the last bit of other days. A lot of runners hate walking with me because of the awkward pace I tend to use, but Miriam drew me along like a well-set spinnaker in a following breeze, keeping my bow out of the heavy seas. Joy came to meet us across the Opihi River Bridge, which had pedestrian access just to put icing on the cake of an already great day. I had covered 64.5kms, making that the best day so far and it had seemed so easy. Dave picked Miriam up and whisked her back off to their lives of farming business.

# Day 10

## Temuka to Ashburton

The pattern of the night was now becoming well established. Walking until 6.00pm, cleaning up and eating until 7.00pm, trying to minimise the foot damage until 8.00pm, trying unsuccessfully to get comfortable enough to read until 10.00pm, not being able to sleep because of muscle tremors and spasms until midnight, fitful sleeping filled with vivid dreams and nightmares until 4.00am, giving up the sleep thing at 5.00am, final foot dressing and porridge eating until 6.00am, and then back on the road. I should add that a long-held habit has been reading a bit of the Bible each day, and I found this really encouraging. I read (Genesis 13:17) *'Arise, walk through the length and the breadth of the land, for I will give it to you.'* I looked at my feet and thought 'last night I could hardly hobble to the shower and now I'm planning walk another 60kms'. Somehow during the shivering and trembling in the night, my body had repaired itself enough to carry on. How could this be? I slid two lumps of pedal lava into my shoes and laced them up. The cooker ran out of gas so I had to make do with muesli.

SH1 bypasses the main street of Temuka, but I didn't. I hadn't been there for years and enjoyed walking through the old town. Other 'developed' countries had long since routed major roads around their towns, but the attitude of NZ road planning while still quite juvenile had at least left half of Temuka free of main road traffic. I had walked just far enough from the starting point at the Opihi River for the normal early morning foot pain to be reduced to tolerable levels. I loved to soak up old towns and try to see what their builders had envisaged as they established communities that would outlast the pioneers themselves. I loved the names they gave things, like the Empire Hotel, the Royal Hotel, the Crown Hotel, and one with no illusions of grandeur, the Temuka Hotel. These premises seemed very serious places but I did read that the Empire Hotel had once (in 1914) been prosecuted for serving liquor on Christmas Day, and I smiled at this naughtiness. The Library and Post Office were old stone structures speaking of permanence and solidarity. A local scaffolding business had a giant cut-out of a magpie on the roof and I wondered briefly about throwing a stone at it for old time's sake. I couldn't find a suitable stone so I left the impulse unfulfilled. Of course, I'm much too sensible these days anyway. The old Courthouse had been turned into a museum, I wondered if that meant crime has been assigned to the past?

We were planning to meet Hugh and Betsy, old friends from our hometown of Owaka, in Orari, so I lengthened my stride and headed north. In Winchester, I noted the Winchester Hotel but not Winchester Cathedral, perhaps they are one and the same. I did start whistling the tune of Geoff Stephens' song of the 1960s and trying to keep the depressing words out of my mind: *'Winchester Cathedral, you're bringing me do-own......'.* To balance things out I found reference to Richard Pearse who hailed from Waitohi just a few kilometres from here. It is said of Richard that eye-witnesses saw him maintain powered flight (in an aeroplane) in March 1903 – some four months before the Wright Brothers at Kittyhawk, and it doesn't matter what the truth of this is, locals in these parts will never be convinced otherwise. Richard was another of those annoying people, with a head full of ideas, who refused to let the negativity of others stop him from having a go.

Joy texted me that the Orari meeting had been postponed until 10.00, so I marched on, thinking to get a few more kilometres in, and she could pick me up and bring me back for the morning break. With this in mind I came to the Orari River bridge and quailed at the thought of crossing it. There seemed to be no let-up in the traffic and most of it was heavy. In the end I walked along the outside of the barriers, with nothing to stop me falling but my grip on the rails. I don't recommend this to anyone, I didn't even recommend it to myself, but suffice to say, I made it across alive. A few kilometres along, Joy texted again.

'I've broken down, can you come back?' 'What do you mean you've broken down?' 'It just died; I don't know what's wrong.' 'Sigh!'

As I turned to head back, a wave of dark depression washed over me and I realised my grip on good mental health, was becoming increasingly tenuous. I was in such a fragile mental state that I couldn't deal with a mechanical breakdown, but gradually I felt the calm hand of logic on my shoulder and I knew it was even less Joy's problem. As I set off back, I tried my hand at hitch-hiking, but to no avail, and of course the first obstacle was the Orari River bridge. Bad enough risking life and limb crossing it once, but to do it twice was madness. Fast forward to the little township of Orari, as I was approaching, I saw the camper coming happily along the road, and there was Joy, all smiles, one of her superpowers, and driving into the café carpark. An older couple had stopped to see if she needed help and the bloke, Kerry he was called, looked under the bonnet and found the earth wire had fallen off the coil. Bless you Kerry – and your wife that made you stop! The world needs more people like you.

The break with Hugh and Betsy was a great time, and a lot of reminiscing went on. These two had been an amazing support to us when our family was young, particularly at the time of our daughter's death, such people are not easily forgotten. While we were there, an old acquaintance from my life as a prison officer chanced to be there and we had a catch-up with him too. Joy took me in the now smooth-running camper, back to where I had turned back, and I was 'on the road again', happy and rejuvenated. That is, until I reached the south branch of the Rangitata River. This was another old-style bridge with narrow carriageway and no possibility of 'hanging out'. I found the best gap in the traffic I could and set off with my best race walk, but no sooner had I entered the danger zone than the road seemed to be full of trucks coming from both directions. I made it over but the experience was so terrifying I texted Joy and asked her to meet me at the second

Rangitata bridge and bear me across. I walked up to the bridge and returned 500 metres so the distance had been covered and she gave me a ride to the other end. I walked up to the Ealing reserve and we had a midday break. I started what was to become a happy habit and had an hour's sleep before continuing. Another happy habit was also started there. Joy asked if I'd like a foot massage? I wasn't sure if I did, given that my feet were so sore, but I took off a shoe and offered it to her. The feeling of exquisiteness was indescribable. Just having them touched and a light fingernail caress was all it took. Then Agatha and Rosette started squabbling as to whose turn it was, and how long these turns should be.

The road from there was straight and (to me) featureless but on arriving in Hinds (the place where the houses are deer) there was a small monument declaring that this was the 43rd Parallel, I was making progress. Next came Winslow, and I wondered if there'd be a *'girl my Lord, in a flatbed Ford, slowing down to take a look at me?'* It seemed that was the sort of thing that should happen in Winslow. Finally as I was coming into Tinwald, which is viewed by many as a suburb of Ashburton and SH1 is very close to the main trunk railway line, I stopped to view a goods train coming into town. Any distraction was worth a stop. The train driver slid his side window back and shouted to me, over the clang of the level-crossing bell:

'I've heard about you, mate, I know what you've been up to. Good job, keep it up. We're all rooting for you!'

Well that was a nice way to finish another day. The last 15kms had numbed my mind to there being anyone else who 'knew what I was up to' and it was mightily uplifting. Three death defying bridge crossings are three too many in a single day, but I was still going and still in one piece. We were staying with another cousin of Joy's (she has heeeaps of them) and co-incidentally the 60kms came up on Strava just as I arrived at their gate. Her cousins are always good fun and Dee was no different, as she and husband Ron laughed the evening away with us.

### *Joy Leslie: Things learned on the Great March North:*

7.    *All wires pertaining to the coil, need to be connected to same coil for the camper to keep driving.*
8.    *Sometimes people with skills – see point 7 – just turn up and help. Thanks again Kerry and Heather.*
9.    *Friends from Owaka are always friends. Betsy and Hugh met us in Orari for coffee.*
10.   *Perhaps I could do with knowing more about the camper than jumper cables and waste water removal.*

# Day 11

## Ashburton to Burnham

Lace up on Day 11 was done in the comfort of Dee's lounge, where I was also back on my traditional diet of porridge. Ron was up and about at 5am so we yarned about people we knew and planes he'd flown, and I was on the street by 6am. I wished I had a plane, and could fly one. Might save the feet. The bridge over the Ashburton River had a footpath, oh the bliss of safe bridge crossing. Like the Waitaki bridge the original model had catered for road and rail, built in 1873 it was in operation until the dedicated road bridge was opened in 1939. This had been badly damaged in a flood earlier this year and the signs of ongoing repair were still in evidence. The bridge looked solid but shook alarmingly with the passing of heavy traffic. Compared to yesterday's crossings though, it was just what the doctor ordered. Probably my doctor wouldn't have been impressed with my feet and may have ordered a few days off, so I didn't enquire. In the riverbed below the bridge were thousands of seagulls, doing their version of the soundtrack from Hitchcock's film, 'The Birds'. I watched them for a while, trying to see what they were up to, but there seemed no real concerted activity, beyond making noise and minor position changes. As in Temuka, I chose the old main street for my passage, and wandered slowly through the old shopping precinct. These towns were much better places without the main traffic bedlam, and Ashburton town fathers (or more importantly the town mothers) had done a good job reinstating the old town charm of this area.

North of town, as I passed the Fairton Freezing Works turnoff, I heard an electronic sound emanating from the roadside grass, and after a small search, located an i-Phone. The screen was locked, but displayed that the owner had a meeting in Ashburton at 8.00am. The cover was pink so I guessed a female meeting attender (and phone on the car roof leaver). Besides the phone, the roadside debris was starting to gather in my mind like rubbish blown against a fence. I have always hated things being thrown out the windows of cars, as if it was someone else's job to deal with it. I had decided for this trip not to let it get me down, but get me down, it did. Perhaps it was my fragile mental state, or something deeper. Our own children had learned not to throw rubbish out of the car, on the pain of walking back to pick it up. Each day that I walked, my nerves became more sensitive, I was more aware of my surroundings, colours were much more intense, smells (good and bad) triggered memory download that sometimes brought me to tears, and sometimes made me laugh. The roadside rubbish so long ignored (except when joined by friends – sorry guys) was starting to get me down. I wanted to rail against it, but there was no reachable target for my ire. Once when walking on the street in Invercargill, I saw a car passenger throw a half-full McDonald's milkshake container onto the pavement in front of me, as the vehicle waited at lights. Without real thought, I picked it up and placed it on her lap, and said:

'You dropped this.'

She got such a shock, she didn't respond, and when the vehicle moved on, she still hadn't responded. Maybe she'd reflected on the crass behaviour, or maybe not. What could I do with a family sized bag of KFC waste? Throw it at a passing motorist? The fast-food giants seemed to use packaging as advertising, perhaps to show the world how stupid their customers are. A new study has shown, (I just wanted to start a sentence with that line of meaningless drivel) that it takes on average, 10 kms of travel by car for a family to consume a meal of fat, salt and emulsifier, wipe their fingers, repack the cardboard, serviettes, and bones in the bag, and throw the whole kit and kaboodle out the window. It's a tight schedule and there isn't really time for consideration of the environment or others who share it. I struggle to see why one would pack the rubbish back in the bag just to throw it out anyway, perhaps I'm missing some vital connection. Tidy littering would be an oxymoron? But then, a litterer personifies the moron part anyway!

The next item of roadside litter pushing its way to the front of my mental filter, was surgical masks. These were turning up in alarming numbers, and given that all deliberate littering is done by stupid people, what does that say of mask wearing, particularly in-car mask wearing? Some roadside debris is accidental and understandable, if not acceptable. Things like ratchet tie-downs, D-shackles and lengths of chain, were often seen, but I understood that the owners of these hadn't wanted to lose them, just hadn't secured them properly. I walked past a small fortune of such items lying in the ditches. The tie-downs were usually damaged and I just made sure they were off the carriageway, but the D-shackles were another matter and I started picking them up and keeping an eye out for the pins. If I could find a matching pair I would put it in the next rural mail-box I came to, assuming all rural people would have a use for a D-shackle and be thankful for this thoughtful gift. I also hoped none of these shackles would fall off a vehicle while it was passing me.

I was walking mostly on the right side of the road facing the oncoming traffic. Technically that's where one should walk, but my experience with the mad texter had left me a bit nervous, of that side. I also changed sides for corners, narrow verges, side winds, steep camber and rough edges. I mainly walked with my head down, watching for roadside obstacles that might cause me to cry, if I stepped on them. Also the wind from big rigs would sometimes blow my hat off, and retrieving it from the water-table was a painful business.

As I was approaching Chertsey, I was walking on the left because there was no verge on the other side, and I saw a tanker approaching. Just as I was about to drop my chin against the wind rush, I noticed a car pull out to overtake the heavy vehicle. The driver seemed to have poor spatial awareness and just kept coming over until the wheels were throwing up dust and gravel from the edge of the verge. As it was coming straight for my knees, I leapt into the grass. There was at least two car-widths between the car and the truck, and as it sped by, I caught a glimpse of a woman with bright red hair, staring eyes, and maniacal face. This was imprinted in my memory, and if I close my eyes, I can still see her, and feel the whip of thrown gravel. I can also hear the angry blast of horn from the truck. When I recounted this to my truck-driving brother, he thought the incident would be recorded on the dashcam and I'd probably star on some TV show some day.

The Rakaia River bridge had been weighing on my mind, and of course that of my safety manager, right from the start of the walk. Since firming up my plan to do this walk, I'd been noticing aspects of the road that didn't suit walking, and this bridge was at the top of the list. There were places more dangerous, but the others were all shorter spans of risk. The Rakaia Bridge was 1.8kms long. More than a mile, and New Zealand's longest road bridge.

Since 1939 when it was opened, vehicles had become wider, faster, and of course, far more numerous. The bridge design was the same as that bridging the North branch of the Rangitata river. No allowance for a walker, or a cyclist. I'd wondered about making the crossing at 2am when traffic was sparse, but the way things had turned out, I was arriving there at midday. Joy had raised the issue a number of times, just in case I'd forgotten that she wanted no part of crossing it on Shank's Pony. I'd fobbed her off, saying I hadn't decided what I would do. This was also my way of dealing with the Auckland situation.

Now I had arrived at the Rakaia, and the bridge had to be faced. While we were having a nice lunch in the camper, parked in the township itself, Gav and Heni, friends from Owaka, pulled up on their way past. It was good to see them and we had a good old catch-up. Gav, who is a mechanic, looked under the bonnet to see if there were any obvious issues after the incident with the coil, the day before. He pronounced it okay, and Joy was happy. I still had some concerns, but this wasn't the time to raise them. I wondered, out loud, if Gavin could tag along for the rest of the South Island anyway, and keep the ancient vehicle on the road. He was gracious enough to consider this for two seconds before saying:

'Yeah, nah.' Which has come to mean 'no!'

They left, and we faced the bridge alone. We decided I would walk up to the bridge approach, then head back South for the 1.8kms to cover the length, and Joy would then transport me over. But before doing that, she wanted a hand to empty the toilet. She had researched the subject and there was a dump station at the local camping ground.

I pointed out that full instructions for the toilet were in the camper manual, but it turns out 'helping her empty it' actually meant doing it myself while she watched. In retrospect, it was probably my job, and I did need a ride across the river.

When these two immovable obstacles (the toilet and the river) were overcome, I hopped out on the North side of the mighty braided river and set off once more. I should have known within a kilometre of the Rakaia, was another bridge over the main trunk railway line. Assumably these were built by railway engineers, with no consideration for walkers, cyclists or horses. It was just as bad as the Rakaia River bridge, but much shorter, so I just took my life in my shaking hands and braved it. It was not a fun experience.

It was 15kms to Dunsandel, where we planned to meet up again, and this stretch was uneventful. No-one tried to kill me, there were no narrow bridges, and it was almost dead flat. I did consider the absurdity of that term for a walker. We went into the café in Dunsandel and had a pie and an ice-cream. These were both tasty, and sitting watching the traffic from the safety of distance was quite therapeutic. It was only at times like this that I realised how much the constant danger of the road, was affecting me mentally. Because Joy already hated the danger, I was putting myself in, I didn't feel I could discuss it with her, and oh, how I needed to.

I had another 10kms to go, and like the last hour of every other day, I hated it. I walked along to the level crossing near the Selwyn river, and thought of the foolishness of these constant railway crossings on a flat Canterbury Plain. The road bridge over the Selwyn had not been on my radar as an unsafe crossing, because it was reasonably modern, but alas, it wasn't safe either. I stood and looked at it, and the almost continual stream of traffic in both directions. There was no safe verge, indeed no safe margin at all. The river itself was almost dry, and I considered going that way, but my feet were in no condition for the scramble down the bank, the rough stones in the river bed, or the scramble back up. I looked at the traffic and noted the south-bound was constant bumper-to-bumper, while the north-bound was not. I chose the left side and when I could see no trucks, just set off across. I had one shoulder hanging as far out as I could manage, and my hip rubbing the barrier. Most cars whipped by without slowing but some braked heavily, sounding their horns angrily. I focused on the task and didn't try to engage with anyone. Some tried to engage with me, with the occasional rude gesture, but I stuck it out. I wasn't sure what the toots were supposed to achieve. Maybe they thought, it needed brought to my attention that I was crossing a narrow bridge.

Finally I was walking past the Burnham Military Camp which seemed to be in total silence. Maybe they were away on manoeuvres, or fighting a war somewhere.

We were to spend the night with Fi and her partner, on Two Chain Rd which runs parallel to SH1. Fi is another runner, familiar with the world of endurance racing. In spite of her lack of stature, she is one of the toughest people I've ever met. I knew I wouldn't have to justify what I was trying achieve here. I knew if I discussed my mental struggle, she's understand. We'd once competed in a Fiordland mountain race called 'Dusky to Dawn' where we'd taken 34 hours to get from Lake Hauroko to West Arm Manapouri. The Dusky Track is a well-known endurance track all on its own, without trying to knock it off in a single go. I'd met experienced trampers that had taken 10 days to complete the track. When we were almost finished, and were walking down the Wilmont Pass road, I asked her if she hated me? She didn't answer for an uncomfortably long time, before relying:

'No, I don't hate you, but I did wonder a few times in the night, about the sanity of us both.'

While driving into Fi's place, we noticed a mare with a new foal in a nearby paddock, and mentioned that to her. Yes, she said it had just been born that very day and didn't even have a name yet. She cooked us a lovely meal, and afterwards, when Joy went off to take a shower, we discussed the road so far. I showed her the mess that had once been my feet. She didn't throw up, or pass out, but I did see genuine concern in her eyes. She asked if I'd considered taking a few days off and getting them looked at? This from someone like Fi, was a question that needed taken seriously. I said I had considered it, but so far had decided to soldier on. As we yarned away, there came an urgent banging on the door. It was a neighbour who had come to tell us, the foal had got itself tangled up in a fence. We all rushed out to deal with this, feet forgotten, shoes jammed back on. The foal had decided to try out its new legs with a bit of a gallop, and this had ended in a tragedy called the fence. I was able to use my fencing skills to cut some wires and release the poor wee beggar. All seemed to be okay, so we went back inside. Joy was a bit bug-eyed when we came in, because she'd come out of the shower and there was no-one about. The place was in complete silence. I said:

'Oh, we've been doing a bit of fencing.'

### *Joy Leslie: Things learned on the Great March North:*

11.  *It is possible to go a whole day without a calamity.*
12.  *We learned how to empty the camper toilet, as in Rog did it and I made encouraging noises.*
13.  *Foot rubs aid circulation, and make the owner of the feet in debt to the foot rubber.*
14.  *I don't have to choose hokey pokey every time for an ice-cream flavour. Today I had maple walnut instead. You can have a day without calamities – but there's always things to learn.*

# Day 12

## Burnham to Waikuku

I laced up my shoes for Day 12 with the news that there were two cases of covid in Christchurch and the city may be in lock-down before the day is over. NZ was still living in the world of fantasy and making believe that lock-downs were a way to combat virus. Christchurch running friends had organised an interview with local media but that was starting to look like a fantasy too. I started work on plans to bypass the city altogether and flee northwards. I had slept better through the night and was a much better place mentally for ignoring foot pain. Agatha and Rosette had brought in reinforcements in that, five days of trying to keep off my heels had created blisters on my toes as well. All 10 were individually taped and I was relying on the medical dictum of 'hoping for the best'. I picked up where I'd left off the day before, at the famous seven road intersection at Burnham, and headed off for the uncertain glow of the lights of Christchurch. Before long I came to the Rolleston Prison, which is situated appropriately enough, on Walkers Road.

My fondest memory of this prison was the day a prisoner had dug up – with a spade – an unexploded mortar round, left over when the site had once been an army firing range. He had taken it to the garden instructor, who, distracted by getting a shipment of vegetables ready for market, had dropped it in a desk drawer and temporarily forgotten about it. This, of course, is straight out of the manual of dealing with unexploded munitions. Later he recalled the bomb and reported it, immediately wishing he hadn't. The Army got a bit excited, cordoned off the area and sand-bagged his little office building, while the device was 'neutralised'. Nobody thought to ask how the device had got in the drawer, or how long it had been there. I wrote a poem about it at the time (see Appendix Two), and using some poetic licence, suggested that the army had dealt with the situation by blowing the office up. This poem, though written tongue in cheek, got into the hands of my superiors and they in turn over-reacted, thinking, among other things, that they had to fund a new garden office. A good opportunity went begging that day.

I carried on towards the Garden City, chuckling to myself as I marched along. It had been suggested to me, more than once, that I was easily amused. I have never denied this, and on these long days, often alone, I found amusement in whatever I could. Joy caught up with me in Templeton, which is close to the Christchurch Men's Prison, where I started my career as a prison officer. She had coffee and a tasty sausage roll for my second breakfast. She went on ahead to Hornby and after parting from me there, promptly got lost. I had given, clear in my view, instructions on how I planned to get through town, but I didn't see her again until Redwood. Bernie, another mad runner, met me in Hornby and walked with me through to Sawyers Arms Road. Much of the conversation was about the covid 'outbreak' and the government's handling of it. A few people were peering with frightened eyes over face masks, but generally it was hard to see that there was anything amiss. The government would not have been happy with this. It's hard to control people who refuse to be frightened. Bernie was, and is always, great fun, and the Christchurch kilometres disappeared quickly. He had heard of my poetry and wanted me to send him some samples, particularly those about the pandemics, past and present.

We met up with Emma further north and she took over the role of keeping me amused, and poking me with a sharp stick every time I looked like wilting. We went round to her parent's place, where lunch was being prepared. Steve and Pam were long-time friends and Joy turned up too for a good old catch-up. She knew where they lived. Steve had also worked in the prisons, and if I'm honest, it was him that talked me into it, back in the day. We had a good laugh about the mortar incident and both felt, as most retired people do, that things were better when we were there.

They pointed me in the direction of the new cycle-way heading out of town and across the Waimakariri River. This new path was fantastic, and as far as my walk was concerned, was the best foot access beside a motorway in the whole country. Lots of native species had been planted and many plaques, spelling out points of interest, were beautifully arranged along the way. Things like the history of the Belfast Meat Works, complete with pictures. Stories of early Māori and how they handled the wetlands and rivers before Europeans arrived. Stories of the Waitaha, who had preceded Ngai Tahu. And finally one that told of the Queen Mary Hospital at Hanmer. This stopped me in my track. It was another tale of our attempts as Kiwis to deal with mental health. The hospital had been established, on the site of the old sanatorium, during WW1 and was for wounded soldiers to recuperate. Soon it was realised that the injuries to the mind were far harder to heal. Then it was realised that alcohol was a serious problem among returned soldiers and the hospital gradually began to focus on alcoholism and addiction. Many were helped with this latter problem, but in spite of this, it was closed in 2003.

I finally crossed the Waimakariri River Bridge with its excellent walk/cycle appendage, and mentally thanked whoever had conceived this futuristic idea – futuristic for NZ – the Dutch and Germans were doing this 50 years ago. Joy was waiting in Kaiapoi when I arrived. She was really on top of her navigational game now. Kaiapoi (food swung – over the wall) is sited near where at first a Waitaha Pa stood and then Ngai Tahu built an even bigger one – perhaps the largest in the South Island. There were great battles and underhand dealings throughout the 1830s before the treaty was signed in 1840. Kaiapoi is quite a beautiful little town and while walking through I noticed the Passchendaele Memorial Path which runs from Kaiapoi to Rangiora. It's good to remember the ugly things of our past, so that we can concentrate on not making the same mistakes again.

Walking north out of town the old main road meets SH1 again near Woodend, and I was 'back on the road again'. I had not been on SH1 since Burnham. My target was the Ashley River Bridge at Waikuku and I had had a full day of walking and talking. As I passed the Pegasus round-a-bout, I wished I had wings too. I could have flown over the Ashley Bridge. Instead, I stopped for the night and we drove back to friends Richard and Heather at Kaiapoi and stayed the night with them. They had a spa so I cut all the bandages off my feet and gave them a good soak. The bandages (and feet) looked like something you might have seen in a Crimean War hospital. It was hard to believe I'd been walking on those feet. There was a lot of conversation on the intended lock-down of Christchurch. The strangle hold of government was closing in on my quest.

### Joy Leslie: Things learned on the Great March North:

15.  Christchurch is a beautiful place in the blossom of Spring, but would be more enjoyable if one knew where one's husband was.
16.  You see a lot of hi-vis as you drive through a city, not all worn by Rog, and I managed to misplace him despite his bright yellow presence.
17.  Coffee with a friend is a great comfort – actually, I knew that already and hospitality of friends is endless.
18.  Not all bridges are walker friendly, so Rog doubled back at the Ashley one to keep kms right, and I will take him over tomorrow.

# Day 13

## Waikuku to Greta Valley

Lacing up my shoes for Day 13 took a long time. When it was done, I was sweating and shaking like a weeping willow in the breeze. The effects of the cold were almost gone, the legs were stiff every morning and after each rest break, but that disappeared 10 minutes into each section, but the feet... They were something else. I couldn't handle any road camber or rough surfaces. Once I got on the road each day, I could assert some mind-over-matter, but first thing in the morning it was definitely matter-over-mind.

This wasn't how I'd thought it would go. I thought, it'll be good for a couple of days, then bad for another two, then I would be away. That was probably true for my legs, but my feet were getting steadily worse with the passing of each day. I questioned myself as to whether 60kms was too much for a day. Certainly, most days I was relatively okay until the 50km mark and then started to struggle to complete the last 10. I was up to schedule, at the current pace I would make it to the ferry in time for my booked crossing, but there was no margin for error, no allowance for vehicle (or mental) breakdowns.

There was too much pressure. I tried to draw from the ultra-races I'd done, there was pressure there too and I had survived, I had overcome, but this was different, this was uncharted water and I was starting to see dangerous rocks beneath the surface. The most dangerous of these was infection in a blister. Both James and Brooke had warned that this was the rock that sinks most multi-day eventing ships. James had said, he'd heard that you should give your shoes the sniff test at the end of each day, because this was the best early warning sign that there was infection in one foot. I wasn't completely sure whether he was kidding about that, so I'd put that advice in my 'pending' file. I decided that from today I would do that. Sniff testing would a part of my daily routine.

After a nice breakfast with Richard and Heather we drove back to the Ashley Bridge. The camper had developed a fan belt squeal, when it was cold, making our passing through the sleeping streets of Kaiapoi less unobtrusive than we'd hoped. This was another niggle to add to all the others, because like my feet, it was a bit worse each day, and like my feet, it probably wasn't going to resolve itself. I suggested to Joy that she drop in to a garage and get the fan-belt tightened. I was struggling with keeping my body going, I didn't have any capacity to deal with mechanical issues, even though these had traditionally been my role in the relationship. It wasn't her fault, though, that her husband had absolved himself from all things non-walking.

There was light rain falling at the Ashley River when we arrived, so for the first time in 10 days I wore my wet weather gear. This lasted only a few minutes and happy, warm sun-shine appeared to brighten my day. Joy texted that a mechanic in Amberley had promised to 'look at' the fan belt in a couple of hours. This was just a small thing, but in my over-burdened mind, it was the lifting of a great weight. The 15kms to Amberley took me well over two hours, but it was a pleasant walk in nice mild temperatures.

As I approached the town, three dogs came out onto a front lawn, to bark at me, which was, as they saw it, their role in life. The larger of the three was their self-appointed leader, but he had one small handicap, he'd barked himself hoarse. He was doing all the actions of a good watchdog, and his mouth was moving with each imagined bark, but there was no sound. I went over to look more closely at this strange phenomenon. If the truth be known, I was probably trying to wind him up, but he started it. Then, when the other two tried to make up for his lack of volume, he ran and attacked them, insisting that he alone had the mandate to bark. He reminded me of Napoleon the Bloodhound in the classic Disney Cartoon, 'Aristocats', who said to his Basset Hound sidekick, 'Wait! I'm the leader, I say when we go....... Now!' We've all met people like that.

I walked right through town looking for Joy and didn't see her. I was going to head on out, when she texted 'Where are you?' She'd been in a gift shop and hadn't seen me go by. She'd scoped a good café for an ice-cream and coffee break. Then we went round to the garage where a suitably old chap (with an English accent) was 'looking at it.' He was a bit nostalgic about 'these good old British motors'. He agreed that the fan-belt needed tightened and proceeded to do it. As he worked, we chatted, and I explained what we were doing. He kindly offered to donate his time and expertise to the venture. There are good people to be found everywhere. Actually, that's not true of everywhere, but it was of Amberley. Looking around I found a statue of Charles Upham, who was twice awarded the Victoria Cross for bravery during WW2. He even did a stint in the infamous Colditz. As I was reading his story, I noted that he was once shot in the foot and carried on in spite of the pain. Later he dug the bullet out himself. Ah, these people that carry on in spite of foot pain. Crazy. Crazy.

There were also three statues outside the Hurunui District Council Office, called the Grandmothers, that were a depiction of the Waitaha people, and carved by one of their descendants. With these things filling my mind, I headed out of town and found the first hill, albeit a small one, in four days. I loved the hills and I hoped my feet did too. I walked past Purchas Rd, and saw in my mind's eye the ostrich farm, a friend had operated along there, during the 'boom and bust' days of this giant poultry. I'd helped him a few times and marvelled at the thickness of these great birds. But, by gum, they could run.

I had been worrying about the Waipara River Bridge, but this was an unfounded concern. There was enough room for me to slip across in relative safety.

Soon afterwards SH7 branched off to Hanmer, the Lewis Pass and Westland, taking with it at least half of the traffic. SW1 was unbelievably quiet and I soaked up the sounds of silence. In the Waipara area I noticed three churches and ten vineyards. It seemed one either had leanings toward the spiritual, or the smooth elixir of the gods.

The rest of the afternoon was spent in getting to Greta Valley about 20kms away. I was loving the variety of the hills and a few corners. Even the bridges were better. Narrow, perhaps, but so short I could stroll across in the leisurely fashion, befitting my age and imagined dignity. At the Greta Village, I saw the camper parked tidily off the road, but saw no sign of Joy. There were public toilets there in the shell of what had been a thriving service station, so I popped in there for a few minutes. There was still no sign of Joy, so I rested for a while, had a wee nap, and finally set off again, texting Joy that I was going to do another 10kms and to pick me up in 90 minutes. She had walked back toward Waipara and missed me while I was in the toilet, and had gone quite a distance before realising the mistake.

As I was winding up to road speed, I noticed a blue Toyota pull up 200 metres in front, and a petite woman hop out. I thought how much she looked like Vicky, a friend and vet from the Taieri back home, whose sheep I periodically shore. She trotted back towards me, and indeed, Vicky it was. All bright eyed and bushy tailed.

'Wow, I can't believe you've got this far' 'Why not? I've been going for nearly 2 weeks.' 'Yes, but it's hundreds of kilometres.'

'No argument there'

'You look in good condition, considering.' 'Thanks, I'm not feeling in great condition.' 'Mate, you're not even limping, you're a tough old bugger!'

'Both feet are so sore there's no point in limping.'

She was running her eyes over me like she was checking a horse out for soundness. She asked questions about my diet, my health, my sleep patterns, my breathing, she even listened to my breathing.

'Yeah, you're a bit broken winded, if you were a horse, I'd be looking at shooting you. It's going to be the knacker's yard for you mate, when you've finished this. By the way, when are you back? I've got some sheep that need trimmed up.'

It was heart-warming that she thought I would 'finish this' and be back. Finally her mum, who was driving the car, gunned the motor with a touch of impatience. Vicky hopped back in, and they were gone, with a rattle of gravel and the smell of acceleration. The road seemed suddenly quiet and lonely. What Vicky lacked in size she made up in exuberance and sheer presence. The happy feeling she left me with, lasted until 7pm when I called it a day. I just kept going until I had 60kms for the day. 400 metres vertical, more than the last 4 days combined. Joy picked me up and we drove back to Greta Valley to camp the night.

### *Joy Leslie: Things learned on the Great March North:*

19.    *Having the fan belt adjusted has stopped the squealing when the camper is cold. Thanks Amberley Automotive guy – he did it for free – and apologies to the residents of Kaiapoi who heard us leaving on Friday morning.*

20.    *Pausing to photograph a cool topiary caused me to miss Rog arriving at the camper from the toilets across the road and I walked about 20 minutes up the road to meet him, except I didn't.*

# Day 14

## Greta Valley to Conway River

Lace-up for Day 14 was more of a happy affair then the previous few days. Maybe the hills had been good for the feet. I let the pressure out of the inflated egos of Terrible Twins and left everything else alone. All 10 toes were now individually bandaged. Brian and Bertie, the two resident bunions, were swollen grotesquely but so far there were no blisters there. Small blessings.

I planned to walk the 17kms from where I'd finished the previous day, to Cheviot, where we would meet for a rest. The 17kms was an estimate and it was a poor one. On previous days my estimations had been good, but this day was not one of those. It was more like 25kms and took most of the morning. The first obstacle was the Hurunui River Bridge, which I knew was one of the few single-lane bridges on SH1, and the only one remaining in the South Island. I couldn't recall how wide it was, but I knew it was long, with a place for cars to pass about half way.

As was my habit I waited for low traffic volumes and then made my attempt. It wasn't as bad as I had feared, because it was a low-speed bridge with steep incline at one end and a sharp bend at the other. In the end, I made it across without difficulty, and there wasn't the usual terror that went with these crossings.

A large truck was growling down the hill, on engine brakes, and would have only stopped with difficulty. The driver acknowledged my standing and waiting, with a blast on his air-horn and a hearty wave. I followed in his wake, and made the passing bay without meeting a vehicle. Then waited there for another gap before the final section.

From there the road stretched on and on without any sight of the hills I knew surrounded Cheviot, and as usual, I was amusing myself with the little quirks along the road. There was a mailbox made of a shearing grinder stand, and as many hours of my working life had been spent grinding my shearing gear, I stopped and had a little reminisce. I could hear the familiar sound and the smell of hot sparks. I could see the ground face of the comb being turned to the light to check for sharpness. Like many things in life, it was worth taking the time to do this job well. I had two complete D-shackles in my bum-bag and I left them there as an offering. Further along the road I came to a little shack standing alone and forlorn by the main-trunk railway line. It was the Domett railway station. I'm not sure what its purpose was, as I doubt any trains stopped there. You certainly couldn't have swung a cat round in there without hitting all four walls. Thinking of this brought on a bout of hysterical laughter. Hysteria, it seemed, was never far below the surface these days. I can assure you though, no cats were hurt as a result of my walk to Reinga, dogs yes, but no cats. I did remove a few cats from the roadway. Cats, whose last thought on earth must have been, 'I can make it, I've got this.'

At the little country service station in Domett, I sat at a picnic table o outside, and reflected on my stupidity at underestimating the distance to Cheviot. Often, during these rest stops, I wanted to lie down, but finding a suitable place was not easy, and the getting down, and more importantly, up again, involved more pain than it was worth. My apple was gone, my two muesli bars were long since eaten and my water drunk. There was nothing for it but to get back on the road.

As I topped the last rise before the Jed River Valley, and Cheviot, my attention was drawn to a top-dressing plane, buzzing around the hills. It would disappear over a ridge, flying light and easy, like a duck coming in to land on a pond, then re-appear, minutes later, on full noise, heavily laden and struggling for speed and altitude. Then, having achieved these essentials, would race across the face of the steep hillsides leaving a feather trail of superphosphate dust in its wake. This aircraft was known as the Fletcher 400 (but known overseas as the FU-24) and had been adapted for NZ conditions by a series of ingenious Kiwi blokes.

The pilots, who seemed to have a high tolerance for danger, would spend their working days landing on steep farmers paddocks, not really designed as airstrips, and taking off again with payloads that had doubled the flying weight of the machines. Then they would fly close to the ground all day, dodging trees and farmers electric fence guy-wires etc. The airstrips tended to be on ridges where stock camped overnight, and dung would fly up off the wheels, adhering to the underside of the wings. My father had once asked the local garage owner, who had flown a spitfire in the Battle of Britain, if he'd considered flying a top-dresser? He had looked at the Fletcher buzzing around the hills and his mind drifted to another place and time, to the war-torn skies over London. He smiled mirthlessly and replied, 'No thanks, I like to have a bit of flying room.' This business of aerial top- dressing, had filled an exciting part of my childhood, that seemed to contain far too few of such things.

Several stars lined up in my childish, excitement deprived sky. Our farm was steep and inaccessible to ground based fertiliser spreading – my father hated flying – the pilot needed to be shown, from the sky, where the farm boundaries were – the aerial guide needed to be small in stature as the cockpit wasn't really designed for two – and so, armed with the self-importance of knowledge someone needed, I was hoisted onto the wing, and clambered in beside the pilot. The pilot was, to my young mind, a superhero beyond any comic book specimen. In the normal hierarchy of families, my older brother would have had this key role, but he didn't care much for flying either. Although, he put it differently, 'Dad gets you to do that job in case the plane crashes. You wouldn't be that much of a loss.'

Filled with these thoughts, I hardly noticed I was approaching the town of Cheviot, until Joy turned up to walk me in. I started rabbiting on to her about top-dressing, flying and Fletcher 400s, and although she listened politely and nodded at each appropriate juncture, she really didn't care. What she cared about, was that she's gone to a motel and purchased a shower and the washing of a load of clothes. She'd also shopped for groceries. All important things, but they struggled for space in a mind, buzzing with Fletchers and the smell of av-gas and phosphate. The bridge over the Jed River had a footpath – well done Cheviot. It was almost midday and I had walked most of the morning without sustenance, so heading into a café was a pretty nice experience. There was a peloton (or plethora, whichever you prefer) of old bikies there too and we had to wait quite a while to be served. I was happy to wait. When the elderly bikers restarted their machines, it shook the little North Canterbury town. Cheviot had almost died as a traveller stopping point during the two years SH1 was closed after the Kaikoura earthquake. It was just starting to rejuvenate itself. I went to the toilet at the café, then immediately wished I hadn't when I remembered that the public loos in Cheviot are adorned with fine wall art, depicting what people look like below the cubical doors.

I decided to do another 10kms before my official midday break, because 24kms just doesn't cut it as halfway in a 60km day. Joy was getting better at selecting suitable spots to park the camper, she had turned it into an art form – far enough off the road to prevent passing trucks from rocking the van – flat, for ease of toilet door opening, and draining all the water from the sink – required distance from last stop (essential) – shade (optimal but not imperative). She was also now using the pre-drive checklist. We had purchased the camper from a helicopter pilot, and he thought in terms of not leaving until you know everything is secure. Once on the road it's difficult to secure the fridge door or ensure the hot tap relief is open. My lunchtime sleep was filled with 'those magnificent men in their flying machines', and I was still whistling that ditty as I set off for the next stretch of highway. Being a hill boy, I was much happier in this area, and glad the plains of Canterbury were behind me.

The bridge over the Waiau River was a relatively modern structure, probably due to the Waiau having a large catchment and therefore, having the occasional periods of rampant destruction. While they had stopped short of provision for cycle and foot traffic, the carriageway was wide enough to allow reasonably safe passage.

The Leader River Bridge was older and narrower but still manageable. Then it was up over the Hawkswood hill, past the old staging post, and into the Conway River catchment. SH1 follows the Conway quite a distance with many opportunities for great river views, opportunities seldom taken when driving a car. I also noticed with a smile the names given to the river tributaries had a certain theme in the Conway Valley, names like Chilly Stream, Cold Creek and Siberia Stream. The pioneer road/rail builders must have thought it was a bit frigid there in the winter, but today was balmy and warm.

When I reached the Conway bridge, I was still short of the 60kms so I carried on up the hill to achieve this. Then we drove down to Claverley Beach and camped the night there. It was our first night sleeping to the rhythmic sound of waves. Joy had been carrying her e-bike on the back of the camper, but so far had not used it. She got it down off the rack and went for a ride. 60kms today with 500 metres vertical – now that's more like it.

### Joy Leslie: Things learned on the Great March North:

21. *Not much going on in Cheviot at 7.20 on a Saturday morning – a bit early for most towns, to be fair. The Number 8 Café has great coffee, and opens before 8.*

22. *I have just filled the water tank in the camper for first time. – as it turns out I should have done it yesterday. It has no system of letting you know that it's getting low. Just runs out. I used to sell reservoir indicators at CCMP – bit of a theme – should have bought one as I left.*

23. *Laundromats aren't as plentiful in Canterbury as in Otago. However, Doug, the nice man at Cheviot Motels was happy for me to use the coin machine there. Go Doug!*

# Day 15

## Conway River to Hapuku

Sunday again. We'd been on the go for two weeks. We were up to schedule and the last 10kms of the day before hadn't hurt as much as usual, maybe the variety of walking on hills really did help. I went through my morning routine, making coffee, reading the scriptures, eating muesli, looking at my feet, dealing with Agro, putting on, and lacing up, my shoes, wait, what? Muesli? Why not porridge? The support manager had forgotten to top up the water tank. We remembered last Sunday and the terse moments we'd had. We resolved not to do that again. There were though, some clouds on the horizon of complete accord. The Hundalee Hills, with the sharp corners (one at 25kph), and the tunnels on the Kaikoura Coast, were worrying Joy, but not me. I took the view that the sharper the corners, the slower the traffic, and therefore the safer the walker. The tunnels too, had corners at each end and one couldn't speed through them. We agreed on a compromise, that she would drive through behind me, displaying our 'Walker' sign and showing her hazard lights. As we left the beach, the sun rose out of the sea, the first time this trip we'd seen that.

The walk up the Hundalees was great and I was in my element. It was Sunday morning, the hour was early, and there was very little traffic. What vehicles there were, could be heard miles away. It was a walker's paradise. Before long, I came on a sign, welcoming me to the

Kaikoura District, and indeed I could see the sea, from SH1, for the first time since St Andrews. I could also see the Kaikoura Peninsula off in the royal blue haze. When one walks 60kms in a day, it is not normal to be able to see that far, but in this spot, I could see beyond my target stopping place. It looked a daunting distance, but I knew I could do it.

I marched happily off down the winding road to the Oara River mouth, where the railway and SH1 come back together. As was typical of railway over-bridges, it was raised, narrow and dangerous, but I was able to detour through a small settlement there and rejoin SH1 further along. This involved crossing railway land, and the sharp metal chips underfoot were not pleasant.

This coastline from here northwards had been devastated by an earthquake in 2016 (7.8 on the Richter-scale). The main trunk railway line and SH1 were trashed and the sea bed in places had been thrust up out of the sea. The recovery work and repairs that were needed were astronomical. It took 18 months to get even restricted access open along the coast road, and as I walked along, I tried to imagine what it had been like. Given the amount of road that had been covered by thousands of tonnes of rock, it was amazing that no one was killed here.

Local Runanga decided that when the road was opened again, there would be traditional records of the hitori rohe (area history) along the shore and that the coast would become a destination and not just a pathway. I came upon carvings and statues that told the stories of those that had gone before. It was quite moving to read stories on these pouwhenua and tekoteko.

The coastline smelled nicely of salt sea where there were sandy beaches, but where it was rocky headland, it smelled of too much sea life spending too much time on shore. I met up with Joy and she had water. It's funny how you don't value something until you don't have it. She had a strange unfathomable look on her face, but I didn't ask.

As I went round to the camper access door, I noticed, first the rubber seal on the side window was hanging down like the eye of a dead possum, then I noticed other signs of damage. Had she been sideswiped by a passing truck? No, it wasn't that. The 'sign of damage' guess, had been a good one. She had been pulling well off the road and had clipped a road sign. She said, she was sure it had moved. Well it is an area with a history of considerable seismic activity, so who knows?

She put the 'Walker' sign on the back of the camper and followed me through the tunnels. It made her happy and it caused no skin off my nose. The nose wasn't the body part that was losing skin. There were road works and new seal from the second tunnel to the Kahutara River, meaning everybody was driving slowly anyway, so the road was becoming progressively safer. As I approached the beginning of the road works, I saw Joy having dialogue with a chap in a contractor vehicle. He was full of that kind of importance that comes from being given unaccustomed authority. His eyes were reflecting the flashing light of his warning beacons. He had been driving up down the new seal section ensuring drivers didn't speed.

'What's that guy doing? Just having a wee stroll up the road, is he?' 'Yes'
'Where has he come from?'
'Bluff' 'Bluff?'
'Bluff!'
'Well I don't think he can walk along here!'
'You're welcome to try and stop him. Be my guest!'
Mr Flashing Lights, said nothing to me as I walked by. He'd obviously not been briefed on what to do with people 'strolling up the road'. Later he drove past me and stopped next to a police patrolman who was sitting there is in his car. I didn't hear what passed between them, and both just looked at me as I strolled past. The policeman looked slightly bemused. Maybe he already knew of me, I never found out.

The Kahutara River Bridge was quite long, and while it didn't have a dedicated footpath, the sides were wide enough to cross it without walking on the roadway. The Kowhai River was similar. Everything was new here. The road from there to Kaikoura was pleasant and wide. The last section of it even had a roadside track. How modern and considerate can you get? This carried on to the top of the hill, where I branched off to drop down to the foreshore of the town. Joy had parked in the public park and we had blue cod for lunch. Now there's some walker food! It was nice sitting there and it was hard to force myself back to my feet, but 'the show must go on.'

North of Kaikoura, I planned another 12kms, but just as I was reaching the Hapuku River, Joy caught up with me and insisted the camper was 'missing' – as in, not running correctly, rather than not knowing where it was. She said it was 'hesitating'. This was not good news, especially on a Sunday, but I could hardly carry on if the main (only) support vehicle wasn't playing ball. I drove it back to Kaikoura and to Joy's relief it repeated the described 'hesitation'. She was of the view that mechanical things tended to play up when with her, then behave perfectly when I came along, but it was being even-handed today.

We went to a NZMCA park and I set about cleaning out the fuel filter just in case it was something simple like that. I hoped for better things in the morning, now for the camper as well as my feet. 50kms for the day, a bit disappointing but still on schedule. 565 metres of climbing. A call from Steve in Christchurch, to make sure we were okay, was a great comfort, but the thunder clouds of impending doom were gathering on the horizon of my fragile mind.

### *Joy Leslie: Things learned on the Great March North:*

24. *The beaches round Kaikoura are beautiful - to look at, not to walk on, or write 'Joy was here' on. Black grit rather than the lovely sand of the Catlins.*
25. *When guys over 50 look under the bonnet of our camper, they sigh in a fond, nostalgic way and say 'Ah, an old Rover'*
26. *VERY DIFFICULT to find the dump station for waste water in Kaikoura.*
27. *The rugged Kaikoura coast is gorgeous but not walker friendly. A guy driving back and forth in a work truck on the worst bit that had just been sealed, was incredulous. "He's just having a wee stroll up the road, is he?" – but in a cool Indian accent. "Yes" said I. What else could I say?*

# Day 16

## Hapuku to Wharenui

Lace-up on Day 16, after a poor sleep due to mechanical worries, was a bit premature. The camper wouldn't start. Hoping for a quiet get-a-way at 6am, I wound the battery into numb submission without the motor firing up. Normally I'd be able to soak up a set-back like this, without a quibble (although this view may not be fully acquiesced by my family) but not on day 16 of my walk to Reinga. My fragile state of mental stability evaporated as if it had never been. I sat staring out the front windscreen, gripping the steering wheel with white-knuckled ferocity. My threadbare plans for the trip had no contingency for not having a support vehicle. I'd have to wait until the garages were open in town (Kaikoura) so I went back to bed and tried not to melt into a blubbering wreck.

I hopped down and retried the starting process, at 0715 and, glory be, it started. We were back on the road. All was well. As we drove to the Hapuku Bridge, it started to rain, not serious rain, but wet enough. Ha, I had a coat, rain was a minor issue. I splashed my way across the curved bridge and fixed my slightly crazed gaze on Kekerengu, while Joy headed back to Kaikoura for supplies.

It was so good to be walking again, making progress and eating up the kilometres. Around the headland, in Half Moon Bay, there were half a dozen cars parked on the side of the road, like dogs tied and waiting for their owners to return. Out in the bay the surf was dotted with heads.

No-one was actually surfing, just swimming out, and bobbing. A young woman was still at the carpark, struggling into a wetsuit. I averted my eyes while she hopped about trying to get enough bare skin tucked away inside the suit for decency. I offered to zip it but she had a strap on it and was soon ready to go. It was a weird basis for conversation but, no matter:

'Hi! Do you come here often?'

'Not as often as I'd like, but yeah, I get here a bit. Today, the office is on lock-down, so I'm 'working from home!''

'Ha, I'm 'walking from home' I'm from Dunedin but I've walked here from Bluff and am hoping to make it all the way the Cape Reinga.'

'Why would you do that?'

'Why would you surf in the rain?'

'Fair enough, I like surfing and the rain doesn't bother me. You get kind-a wet anyway.'

'Well I like walking and the rain doesn't bother me either.'

'The way you walk, you'll be there in no time. By the way, you should come and surf with us, your body could probably do with a good soak in the sea.'

'Thanks anyway, enjoy your surf!' 'Cheers'.

She tucked her board under her arm and ran barefoot across the road and disappeared down the bank, to join the black dots in the sea. Round a few corners, I came upon Paparoa Point Scenic Reserve, and was impressed with the beautiful job done by the road crews who had dealt with the aftermath of the 2016 earthquake. Out of ruins had come something quite special. Well worth stopping for a look. I thought of the rugged coastline and the people who had worked (and died) here putting the railway line in.

I read that over 1,000 labourers had lived in 22 temporary camps between 1936 and 1945. These were war years too, and must have been stressful times. Many of the men would have had families somewhere but this was the only work available. Eight of them had died doing this and there was a plaque at the Kaikoura Railway Station commemorating them. When you take the train or drive your car around these sheer bluffs and narrow corridors between mountain and sea, you really don't think much of what went into providing that privilege. When one is walking though, there is more time to reflect, to smell the sea, to hear the distant voices of the past and the sound of tunnels being blasted out of rock. A lot of effort has now gone into protecting both road and rail from further rock falls, something we walkers appreciate. Space has been left in various places for parking, encouraging drivers to stop and look, or photograph, this amazing place. I saw a sign stating that the seal colony was temporarily closed – I wondered if the seals knew that?

Joy was parked at Nin's Bin, Rakautara, and I was happy to have some more seafood, for that's what Kaikoura means. There was a nice public toilet there and the wall was covered in ceramic tiles depicting drawings from school children from the area. It was a nice touch and I dawdled longer than I otherwise might have.

At Karaka there's a café specialising in Cray, and there's a larger-than-life specimen on the roof. This brought to mind the Fred Dagg song 'We don't know how lucky we are', and this set me off singing about Bruce Bayliss.

Later in the morning I came to the Clarence River (Waiau Toa) also with a curved bridge, and paused for while staring at the silver-coloured water rushing down to the sea. The Clarence drains the Molesworth Basin, many kilometres away through the mountains, where once the biggest sheep station in NZ was farmed. I had competed in half a dozen ultra marathons in the Molesworth, often walking beside the Clarence (or the Acheron that flowed into it) and I seemed to have quite an affinity for the ice-melt waters. The annual event used to also hold a bard competition, which of course attracted my attention (see appendices three and four – *Running Through the Rainbow* and *Wind in the Willows*). I'd done a lot of suffering and eaten a lot of dust on the banks of the Clarence. I wondered how long the water took to run down from the Rainbow to the sea at the SH1 Bridge?

The stretch of road from the Clarence to Kekerengu was flat and featureless, making my feet hurt and the road and rail builders had not had any trouble here. There used to be many fords, over creeks in this area. Most written history speaks of not being able to get through when it was raining. Small insignificant trickles turned into raging torrents without warning. Sometimes it wasn't even raining on the coast. Farmers in the area were used to having folks to stay, who were caught between the fords.

Some more enterprising chaps made a bit of coin on the side, pulling cars through, or out of, the creeks. There are no fords now, the last one being bridged around 20 years earlier. Another thing that went a few years ago is the Service Station at Kekerengu, making the piece of road without fuel or service, between Kaikoura and Ward, quite a long stretch.

I decided to go on from Kekerengu to Wharenui, and go for the 60kms in spite of the late start. The toes on my left foot were starting to hurt, more than they had, and this added to the constant strain I was under.

Joy picked me up about 10kms past Kekerengu, and we returned there for the night. On the way, the camper got up to its old tricks again, just in case I was planning a nice relaxing night. There were good toilets and showers at the camper park, so at least I would be able to toss and turn all night in a clean state.

When I unlaced my shoes, I sniffed them individually, as per advice from James, and the wisdom of this was suddenly a thing. My right shoe smelled, as it always did of stale sweat and old socks, but the left one had the smell of rotting seaweed. I redid the smell test, and there was no doubt, I had some infection in my left foot. I cut off the bandages, and the three smallest toes were swollen and oozing unpleasantness.

There I was, sitting in a camper that was becoming more of a liability as the days went by, and looking at a foot that would probably need professional help. Joy looked at the toes with the big eyes of concern, but remained silent. She could put a lot of feeling into silence. Then I heard the sea murmuring in the recesses of my mind and I remembered the conversation with the surfer that very morning. She'd said: 'You could do with a good soak in the sea.'

The idea of walking down the beach in the condition I was in, brought the sweat of panic out on my forehead, and did not appeal. The

Kekerengu beach was steep with heavy dark gravely sand. Then I had a brainwave, Joy was fit and able bodied, and bursting with helpfulness. I asked if she could pop down to the sea and fill the 3-litre bottle? Off she went and was gone quite a long time, then returned with the water, but with a lot of attitude to go with it.

'Look at me! I'm soaked' And she was – only her shoulders and head were dry.

'You're speaking like this is my fault.' 'It IS your fault.'

'You only had one job; how hard could it be?'

'Well, next time you can find out, because I'm not doing it again!' 'Hey, you're dripping all over the floor.'

'Do you want this poured on your head?'

I didn't, so I thanked her for the water that had come at such great personal cost, and brought it to a hot, but tolerable temperature, on the gas stove. Then poured it into a basin and put both my feet in there. It was bliss and I left them there for a couple of hours, reheating the water a few times, to try and extend the bliss.

In spite of all the things that had gone wrong, I'd still managed 60kms for the day. All I wanted for Christmas was that the camper and feet would all be working in the morning. It wasn't too much to ask. Was it?

***Joy Leslie: Things learned on the Great March North:***

28. *Disconnect the battery before cleaning the fuel filter. Auntie Google and You-Tube say so.*
29. *Ask Auntie Google before the deed.*
30. *Prolonged, unsuccessful attempts to start vehicle at 6 am among sleeping campers sounds very loud.*
31. *Prayer, and going back to bed for a while, are both good things. On the road by 7.20am. Camper running sweet.*
32. *This thing we are doing doesn't make your feet pretty.*

# Day 17

## Wharenui to Weld Pass

I awoke at 5.00am to the camper being buffeted by strong winds. As I gingerly got down, my feet were sore, but not as bad as I'd been expecting. Was I imagining it? I desperately wanted them to be better. I set about applying a new set of bandages and talking nicely to each toe and heel in turn. Even the terrible twins were subdued. At 6.00am I tried the starter and, it was, 'shake of the head, no go'. I asked another camping couple if they could assist me with a jump start boost, but they weren't the helpful kind. The woman said 'We've helped people before, and they weren't in the least bit grateful.' A pox on the ungrateful helped.

Another day was rapidly going down the gurgler. I had two days and two nights to get to the ferry and 100 kms on the hoof between me and that all important terminal. I needed terminal velocity. I could walk nights, if I needed to. If only I could get on the road in the next couple of hours, but it wasn't looking good. The sound of traffic on the highway tantalised and mocked me. They were getting where they wanted to go, doing what they wanted to do, while I was shackled to the spot by broken machinery. We waited until a decent hour and phoned the AA. Their phone-in system is a tick box exercise and if one's problem doesn't fit the categories, that's too bad.

'What is the nature of your problem?'

'My campervan won't start; I think it's a problem with fuel.'
'Camper won't start, we'll send someone to assist in starting.'
'Could I speak with the mechanic?'
'No, a mechanic will be with you in approximately one hour.' 'Sigh'.

The mechanic arrived around 9am, having driven all the way from Kaikoura. He had no diagnostic equipment or fuel with him. He was told we needed a jump start. He had been born into, and trained for, a world in which there were no old Rover V8 petrol motors. He had no idea what was wrong with it, or how to go about finding out, but suspected more fuel would have helped. If only he'd known that, he could have brought some with him. He organised a tow truck from Blenheim, 70kms away to the North. At least it was in the right direction.

Joy wasn't overly happy with the idea of being left there to deal with the towage, but she could see her crazy old husband was only one combination door away from the secure ward at the hospital.

I set my pigeon brain for Blenheim and after a couple of circles, I was off, carrying enough food, money and clothing for the whole day. I knew there would little roadside assistance, and certainly no foot massages. I was still convinced the infected toes were better after the hot sea water bath, but only time would tell. The first 10kms were a repeat of the last portion of yesterday's walk, but I was moving. The wind was blowing coldly and fiercely behind me, but it was dry. I had chosen this time of year, for the mild temperatures and southerlies of the equinox, and that day those winds found me. I thought how Joy would, at least, be glad she wasn't driving the camper in such blustery conditions.

I was watching out for the tow truck and saw one heading south in the form of Trev's Towing. The brief glimpse I had of 'Trev' assured me he knew what he was doing, and sure enough, after another hour, the same truck passed me heading north with our sad old camper on the back. Trev gave me a friendly toot on the way past, and I was suddenly overcome with loneliness. So much of the success so far had been down to the support I'd had, and now I was alone. I sat down in the roadside grass and couldn't keep back the tears. Slowly I descended into state of self-pity and hopelessness.

I finally got up and angrily set off again. Crying in the grass was getting me nowhere, but I did feel better after walking off the mood. I soon passed the sign welcoming me to Marlborough and another assuring me it was only 80kms to the ferry. In spite of everything, I was still making progress.

The physical wind was buffeting my back and flapping my high viz jacket, but the mental wind was against me. I was beating into it, trying to sail off a dangerous lee shore. My own Great, Great, Grandfather, Captain Charles Hayward, who had been harbour master at the Catlins River Mouth, had lost his life trying to do the same thing in a storm off the rugged Catlins coast. I was no sailor but I understood the principles of sailing. I was sailing as close to the wind as I dared and only just managing to keep off the rocks with each desperate tack. I stopped at the St Oswald's Church and read of the efforts to restore this historic building after it had been damaged in the recent earthquake. It had originally been built in 1927 by some grieving parents in memory of their son. I'd have liked to have talked with these people about their loss, and what it's like to lose a child. I'd have also asked what the support systems were like in their day?

Finally I crossed the Ure (Waima) River where SH1 leaves the sea and heads directly north into the hills. It was nice to be in the hills again. I was mostly enjoying the wind, but it became dangerous when it was joined by the shock wave of a large truck. On one occasion, I was blasted from my feet, and added a bleeding knee to my list of woes. One thing about having so much foot pain, was that minor scratches just didn't cut it as serious issues.

I had my midday break at the café in Ward. The staff at the café there, were surprised to see me come through the door when there was no vehicle outside. I explained my mission and they kindly gave me a free coffee. Nice people, and such coffee always tastes better. I remembered once attending a funeral in Ward and visiting the War Memorial Hall afterwards for refreshments. The plaque at the front named those who had given their lives in the 1914-1919 Great War. I pointed out to the officiating minister that the war had ended in 1918. He winked and said 'Keep your voice down, the returning soldiers took quite a while to find their way back home and had misled their womenfolk as to when the action had actually ceased.'

I was alarmingly tired. The continual buffeting of the wind, coupled with the fact that I was walking faster. Seeing I had started so late I had decided to lift the pace to 7kph. It was all taking a heavy toll. One particularly savage blast of wind blew my hat into the water-table and while this wouldn't normally have been anything more than a mild irritant, on this occasion it was a disaster. My feet and body were in no condition to climb down the steep bank, and more importantly back out again. Trouble was, I was emotionally attached to the hat. It had travelled the whole road with me. I finally retrieved it at great physical cost, but was immediately glad, as I pulled it firmly onto my head.

The road then wound past Lake Grassmere, NZ's largest salt extraction facility. I sat down on a small platform that may have once been a cream stand next to a number of rural mailboxes at the end of Marfells Beach Road. There must have been many houses down that road. I had collected 4 D-shackles that day, and so the nearest boxes each got one. I looked at my feet and thought of the seeming improvement after bathing in that same salt as I could see piled in massive heaps across the bay. The feet may not have actually been better, but at the time, thinking they were, was all important.

Between Grassmere and Seddon I crossed a dangerously narrow little bridge over the Blind River. I wasn't sure of the background of this name but it was certainly appropriate considering the visibility at the end of the bridge. Making things much worse, on this day was the wind. I hadn't realised how much I'd come to rely on my acute hearing to read the presence, direction and speed of traffic. In the wind I could hear almost nothing and vehicles just appeared, apparently out of nowhere. The state of my feet also meant it cost me dearly each time I stopped and looked around.

Seddon was a welcome relief, from wind, traffic and exhaustion. I limped painfully into the excellent public toilets. Can public toilets be excellent? Indeed yes, just try the alternative! It took me quite a long time to finish my business, because for one thing, I was out of the wind, and I was sitting down. I had been dreaming of some sort of treat in

Seddon. An ice-cream, a chocolate bar, a pie, a Jimmy's Pie perhaps? But I didn't feel like it. I needed Joy there to tell me what to do. To tell me I needed to eat. I'd known that I'd been leaning on her in so many ways, but until days like this one, I didn't know how much. I texted her to say I'd do another couple of hours, and would then need a pick-up, probably somewhere near Weld Pass. Afterwards, I admitted to myself, that the text was just a ruse, to reach out and connect with someone. I was rapidly turning into a blithering wreck. No matter what the immediate future held, I wouldn't do any more days on my own.

I knew something of the history of Seddon but I didn't seek any more. I had no capacity to absorb information, to find out about people who'd been here before. The town had been named after Richard 'King Dick' Seddon, as Ward had been named after one of his parliamentary colleagues. Seddon was NZ's longest serving Premier and had been something of a domineering character, he probably deserved a town.

I headed out of town, unsure as to whether I could actually do two more hours, but I wouldn't die wondering. I had been looking forward to the Awatere River crossing with its historic road/rail bridge, and I wasn't disappointed, it was just as I remembered, driving across the single lane bridge under the tracks.

As I had at the Clarence River, I stood and gazed into the waters below, knowing they had come from the north-east end of the Molesworth Station, and had run off some of NZ's wildest non-forested country. That river could tell a few tales. At the Awatere Valley turnoff, there were signs warning of the dangers of the road through the Molesworth, but today the status was 'Open'.

Our daughter Hannah lives in Blenheim, with her husband Kent, who came to pick me up at Weld Pass. He seemed slightly incredulous that I had made it from Bluff in only 17 days. I think he was also a bit alarmed at how shattered I looked, but he kept that to himself. He's a barrister and knows how to keep control of his facial expressions. I'd started late in the morning, and had still managed 60kms, and at 689, it had been the second most vertical metres in a single day, so far. No wonder I was so munted.

On the trip into Blenheim, I got a text from the Inter-Islander.

'Due to mechanical failure of the ferry Aratere, your booking has been cancelled. You can reschedule for a later sailing. Please visit our website!'

Sigh!

I love a bit of irony. Awatere means 'quickpath'.

It was great to see Hannah, and natter with her, out of the wind. By this time though she was firmly on her mother's side regarding what steps should be taken from here. Probably should forget the rapidly closing North Island and just head down the West Coast.

**Joy Leslie: Things learned on the Great March North:**

33.  I have learned so many things that I needed a cup of tea and a sit down.
34.  All those AA subscriptions you have paid in your lifetime - sometimes pay off.
35.  Tow truck drivers have skills, and Trev of Trev's towing was really nice as well.
36.  Side of the road diagnostics aren't always correct. Learning to disbelieve your fuel gauge is much simpler/cheaper than replacing your fuel pump. It will never be allowed to get below half again.

# Day 18

## Weld Pass to Koromiko

Lace-up for Day 19 was pretty relaxed. I had until 3.00pm the next day to get to Picton, and only 40kms to cover. We had stayed the night with Kent and Hannah and it was a great catch-up. The camper was sitting smugly in the drive, with a 'Who? Me?' look about it. Trev the towy had dropped it off the day previously, at a place called Motor- Kanix. They had deduced that it was only a shortage of enough fuel to start. What a drama free end to a dramatic day. As a firework, it was a fizzer. Somehow, I doubted that this was the end of it, but a simple solution was fine with me. The normal me would have been extremely sceptical, but the road-walking me nodded and forgot about it. Joy drove me out to Weld Pass, and because it would only be a short day, I wasn't even worried about my feet. I was still convinced the infected toes were on the mend, but in my current condition I was a poor example of a reliable sports medic.

The weather was still windy and cold, as I made my way into Blenheim. I didn't care, I was unaccountably happy. Joy hadn't driven by; she must have decided to read a book for a while. Why not? She'd been with Hannah for half a day, the chances were high that she would have several more books now, in her private library. These two girls didn't agree about everything but they both liked to read and there was an obvious solidarity in their opposition to the self-destruction they saw in me.

As I came into Riverlands, I noticed a group of Pacific Islanders working in a roadside vineyard. There was a vehicle sitting nearby with a port-a-loo trailer hitched to it. A white overseer was sitting in the vehicle watching them. None of them looked happy. The workers were dressed in heavy coats and woolly hats but still looked to be cold. I stopped and called to them:

'I thought you guys would be singing.'

Ten black faces with big white smiles popped up from among the vines, and their spokesman replied, in a rich baritone:

'It's too cold. You can't sing when it's cold!' 'Yes, it certainly isn't warm.'

As I walked away, all eleven of us were happy. I had broken the cold monotony of their day. Only the overseer wasn't happy. He glared sourly at me as I departed. How dare I hold up the production by reaching out to his workers. I wondered who cared about the mental health of these men? Families far away on the islands. Doing tedious work that New Zealanders didn't want to do. Perhaps I was being unfair and there were people here who cared about the welfare of these guys. I hoped so.

I heard the burble of the rover V8 and Joy cruised by, pulling up in front of me. She said the grey water tap was broken and she was going back to the Motor-Kanix guys to see if they could fix it. I carried on walking through the streets of Blenheim, and passed a camper dealership called Deluxe RV Group. I obviously wasn't included in this group. Some examples were selling for $250,000 (only $230k more than my budget), mind you, they probably weren't breaking down every other day and needing towed into town.

When I turned up at Motor-Kanix, our camper was up on the hoist and repairs were being made to the grey water outlet. Somehow in the confusion of the garage experience, I left my coat there. It wasn't a 'no coat' day, and I was soon to regret this oversight. In some places and times, this kind of mistake would have been fatal. It was sunny as I headed over the twin rivers (Taylor and Ōpaoa) but this was not to continue. The bridge over the Ōpaoa had been on my mind. The old structure had been famous for its narrowness. This main artery between the ferry and the rest of the South Island had a bridge which, if two wide vehicles turned up there together, one had to back off before either could progress. The planners of the new bridge had decided to leave the old one for cycle/foot traffic. What had once been known as a bottleneck was now the widest foot bridge in NZ, and I zig-zagged across it, just because I could. A sheep, particularly a feisty sheep, when faced with the restriction of a gateway, will often jump as it runs through. That was me, that day in Blenheim. A mental jump, you understand.

On the northern bank there was a tall, striking pouwhenua, a carving depicting the journey of the peoples who had had lived in this area.

As I set off for the hills, the weak sunlight disappeared, and it got cold with spots of rain. I thought about going back for my coat, but my feet were against this and thought I'd probably be warm enough once I got moving. Once I stopped reading plaques and pouwhenua etc. There is a dedicated footpath along-side this stretch of SH1 and I normally would have enjoyed this, but I was 'too cold, you can't sing when it's cold.' I started looking for shelter from the wind and hating the open stretches. I thought of the trampers and runners over the years who had died, thinking they could outrun hypothermia. One of the things hypothermia does, is mess with your power to think and reason. My thinking and reasoning department were already skating on very thin ice. Hypothermia is something others have, people in the mountains, far from shelter and help, not someone walking within a few kilometres of a large town. Particularly a town in which my own daughter had a nice warm house. I knew there was a shop at Spring Creek, maybe I could warm up there. But I didn't have any money, so I passed through town and walked off into the wilderness of cold.

I reached the Wairau River bridge (Bridge 0201 whatever that means) and my cold addled mind was asking whether Bridge Crossing 201 was perhaps a tertiary qualification? I made it across unscathed, traffic was light, perhaps caused by the cancelled Cook Strait ferry. I was now shivering uncontrollably, and as I came into Tua Marina; I noticed some large but dead harakeke bushes on the side of the road. I did what I should have done a lot sooner. I burrowed into the shelter of the flax, and with numbed fingers, I texted Joy.

'I need help, I'm freezing.'

'Where are you?'

'Tua Marina.'

She turned up in no time and the warmth of the camper reached out and embraced me. She cooked a delicious lunch and I slowly returned to the happy world of being warm and fed.

After a nice midday kip, I was off again, with my coat. Heading for Koromiko, which would leave 10kms to reach the ferry terminal the next day. I was back in the hills again and enjoying myself. A silver SUV passed me and pulled up along the road a bit. A man got out and started walking back towards me. Closeness brought recognition and it was Alvin another old friend, and his wife Victoria, from Milton. Both were builders, he of boats, she of children, in her role as a teacher. We discussed the lack of mental support for teachers. More and more, was being required of them, seemingly with less resources in the support area. The resources seemed to be getting eaten up by an ever-growing Head Office in the Department of Education. They had been following my progress, but hadn't known of the mental struggles. They said my posts looked like it was a breeze. That's how it is with mental health, isn't it? Things looking rosy on the outside, while on closer inspection, that beautiful bush is full of thorns.

When I reached Koromiko, I saw there an old church called 'St John's in the wilderness.' Maybe the Tua Marino River had once been the Jordan, or perhaps this was a reference to the closing of the famous cheese factory that had been here since 1895, leaving the area a bit bereft.

A little later I met Joy, driving nonchalantly along, but returning from the other direction. She had popped through to Picton, 'just to see how far it was.' She was a bit miffed.

'Where's the sign saying this is Koromiko?'

'There's the airport right over there.' I had told her Koromiko is where the airport is.

'That's the Picton Airport!' And so it was.

We drove back to Blenheim to spend another night there before the ferry crossing. I got another text from Interislander, that the booked crossing would now be 3pm. It looked like there would be no walking on the Wellington side tomorrow. 32kms for the day. For the second day running, my feet were no worse than the day before. Could this be the big turning point of my body's deterioration?

We went out for a meal with Kent and Hannah, our first restaurant meal in 20 days. When we got home, we watched the news, and The Prime Minister was announcing the Red-Light lock-down of Hamilton and the Western Waikato, with closed borders. Reinga was looking further and further away. I had, right from the beginning, had as plan b, turning left at Picton and going via Nelson, down the West Coast and back to Invercargill. Friends and family were advising me to take this option. 'You'll never get through the North Island now!'

I would decide when I got to Picton. Tomorrow. The 'cras' in procrastination is Latin for tomorrow.

I read in Proverbs 26:13 The lazy say, 'there is a lion on the road, a fierce lion in the streets.' I'd proved I wasn't lazy, but was I stupid?

**_Joy Leslie: Things learned on the Great March North:_**

37. _To me from a distance, I thought fondly of an ice-cream cone, – see photo below – flavour to be chosen. Alack and alas, it's a golf course._

38. _$2 coins rule when you're camping. One for a shower, two for a load of washing, and, a new one today, to open the lid on a dump station so that grey water – or toilets – can be emptied. Thought it had been closed and had to ask._

39. _The merino insoles that I bought in Clinton on Day three, are great in my sandals from two summers ago._

40. _The tablet that we bought especially for the trip, goes now that we've got a cord for it._

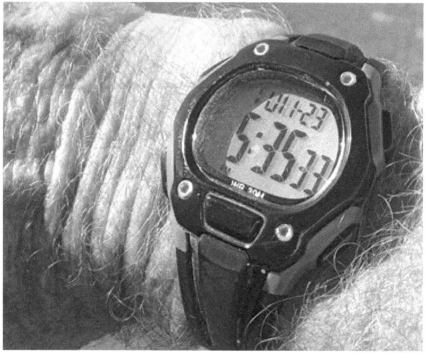

# Day 19

## Koromiko to the Ferry

Lace-up on Day 19 lacked the drama of other days, that had become as much a part of my life as breathing. I had only 10kms to go to the ferry, and all day to do it. The way the ferry schedule was going, we would be lucky to get across without further delays. I discussed taking an earlier sailing and leaving Joy to bring the camper over when she could get on. This was met with a cold stare. Not ostentatiously so, but it was definitely there. I was back to accepting the day as a complete loss, which would have to be made up in the North Island. Still, I had completed the lion's share of the South Island in 18 days.

Even with the road from the ferry to Reinga being 100kms further than SH1 in the South Island, I was up to schedule and should perhaps see this set-back as a needed rest. Perhaps. It was like sitting too long at an aid station during an ultra. It was probably good for you, but you had a nagging thought that you were throwing away all the hard work.

Kent and Hannah helped us do another thing we should have done a lot earlier, design a flier to hand to people who asked and wanted to contribute to the cause. They printed out a number of copies and we stashed them in the camper, and I took a few in my bum-bag.

Back in Koromiko, I hopped out of the camper to another blustery day. The normal V8 burble, as Joy left, was snatched away by the wind. As I walked and got into my stride, I was assessing my feet for improvement or deterioration. I was sure the infected toes were better. I was an experienced sufferer of infection. For most of my 66 years every cut and open injury had got infected and required further treatment, but this time it felt better. Toes crossed. I was just starting to get my second wind, when I saw a golf ball bounce high off the road and then into the water table. I hadn't noticed until then the Picton Golf Course on my left, and went to retrieve the ball. Two hardy old blokes were standing at a Tee and looking in my direction. The wind made conversation impossible, so I threw the ball back onto the fairway. I'm not sure what sort of penalty this would have incurred, but I wouldn't imagine it was a tournament day. They waved their thanks, and then I noticed more balls on the roadside, so I threw them back over the fence too. Recycling, always recycling.

As I walked along, I heard above the wind a high-pitched torturous sound that I couldn't place. My hearing had become refined. I could tell what sort of vehicle, which direction, how fast and how big. I could tell a vehicle with a trailer, from those without. This ability was seriously reduced when there was wind, and I was in more danger on days like these.

As I stopped to try and place the strange sound, a commercial utility screamed by from behind me, towing what looked like a generator trailer. When I say 'screamed' I mean screamed. The jockey wheel was still down and being towed along the road. The wheel itself, which had no doubt started the day as a full-sized unit, was now just an axle hub, and turning at revolutionary speed. Somebody would have some explaining to do at the end of this trip. This brightened my day, not because I revel in damage, but because I had been a contractor myself and could imagine the excuses that would follow the discovery of the missing wheel. 'Didn't you hear any sound as it thrashed itself to death?' Nah, there was nothing, must have fallen down after I started.' Right since the journey began at Bluff, I had dreamed of walking down into Picton, and it was as nice as I thought it would be. I'd done 992kms by road, climbed 6,584 metres of vertical and spent 156 hours on the hoof, at an average of 6.36kph.

Just the North Island to go. A North Island that was being slowly strangled by government movement restrictions. There was now talk about Wellington also going into Red. I just needed to get over there and get moving, maybe under the cover of darkness.

A large white tractor unit was sitting on the side of the street in Nelson Square, and the driver hopped down to meet me. He looked like he had been waiting for me. He had:

"I've seen you three or four times over the last few days, and everybody is talking about you on the blower. What are you up to?"

'I'm walking from Bluff to Reinga, raising money and awareness for Mental Health. It's taken me 19 days to get here.'

"Shit, 19 days from Bluff, that's outta here! Do your feet hurt?"

'A bit, yeah well, actually quite a lot.'

"I have bi-polar, and I've always struggled to hold a job down, but my current company, and particularly the boss, are really understanding. I'm starting to believe for the first time in my life, It's okay to be me."

'Absolutely, it's okay to be you. I wish there were more bosses like your one.'

"Well thanks for doing the hard yards for us."

As I walked off down the street to the Ferry Terminal, I saw the Picton School and thought, 'I've got the time to go and talk to the kids.' I googled the school, found out their number, and gave them a call. The lady who answered said it sounded like a good idea to her, but she'd ask. She called back in less than a minute and said: 'yes, we'd love you to come in, where are you?'

'Standing outside in the street.' 'Come on in!

The school had a security fence similar to Rosebank School, in Balclutha. Perhaps they had a student with Down Syndrome too. Finally I managed to crack the code (open the security gate) and go in. The principal met me, thanked me for the visit, and took me to a classroom where a teacher had had less than five minutes warning of the change to his teaching plan. If he was upset, he hid it well. He Introduced me and informed the children, they didn't have to be a part of this, but it would be great if they were.

About 20 children looked keen and gathered around, while the other 10 faded back to the edges of the room to sit this out. As the talk went on, one by one, the others had an attack of FOMO and drifted nonchalantly back to be a part of the discussion. These were Year-8 students with an amazing capacity to reason and absorb information. Question time got more and more lively with some really well thought out ideas being offered. Sadly, we had to bring it to a close, as the school day was finishing, but the teacher wanted me to hang about, to discuss the subject further. I went back to the foyer and waited. The principal came along and thanked me and as he was doing that the class teacher turned up all abuzz. He told the principal that the children had been more animated about this presentation than anything covered in the last year of disruptions. He said the children were in limbo, as if they were waiting for the real show to start, not realising this was the real show. He said people like me, with the dust and grime of the road on their shoes, should be invited into schools across the land to talk about the real-life issues. I was assuming the 'dust and grime' reference was a metaphor for 'out there doing it', but I stole a look at my shoes anyway.

As I walked back out the gate, which was easier to open from the inside: I was glad I'd not followed my first impulse to just walk on by. The conversation with the children was very rewarding, and uplifting. One girl had asked if I thought she could do the same thing, and what she could do to prepare for it? I said 'Invest in good friends.'

Joy was parked in Lane 4, of the ferry queue, which would now be sailing at 8pm. She had been talking to the ticket girl who said, what we were doing made her day. She was so glad to finally hear a 'good news' story.

At 8:30pm the ferry got under way. Wellington was still open, but the media driven fear was slowly suffocating the North. Advice from friends was to stay in the South Island. "You'll never make it to Reinga, probably won't get past Taupo, that's if you even get through Wellington.' But here we were, on the ferry, sailing off into the darkness. A hired security guard came and asked me to put my mask on. I went and purchased some coffee. It can take a long time to drink coffee, up to three hours, I'd heard. We arrived after midnight. We were in the North Island.

### *Joy Leslie: Things learned on the Great March North:*

41. *Don't make rigid time plans when the Cook Strait Ferry is a part of the plan. Finally due to get on. Original booking was yesterday, then 10 this morning.*
42. *If you have to spend a lot of time in a queue, it's rather nice to be spending same time in a camper. Also, with no reflection on our precious whanau, nice that there are no children or pets in the mix.*
43. *It was very nice to spend a couple of nights in a real house as variety in our current nomadic lifestyle.*

# Day 20

## Wellington to Waikanae

I laced-up on Day 20, filled with enthusiasm. I was in the North Island, all going well I would be past half way to Reinga by the end of the day. Another barrier, both physical and mental, had been overcome. The swelling in my infected toes was definitely reduced. Wellington had not been locked into a red zone, yet. My plan to sleep on the ferry had been a fizzer, but I was well into 'The Bielski Brothers' and I knew that no matter how bad things got, I was a lot better off than them. Trying first to save their own families and then the hundreds who came to them for help.

The ferry had arrived in to Wellington after midnight, and by the time we drove down onto the dock it was 1am. We drove less than a kilometre and found a park on the corner of Hutt and Kaiwharawhara Rds. The plan was to sleep a few hours and then get moving. As was normal, it was an adequate park for me, but not Joy. 'We'll get arrested if we park here.' She'd read the Bielski Brothers too. It was near the motorway and also on a busy street corner. Wellington never sleeps. Every time a vehicle pulled up at the lights, she was wanting to dress for the impending arrest. Would we get separated in the Police Cells, or could we stay together? There was a lot to worry about. Between these enquiries, I slept like a log. I had made my mind up; I was still on the road to Reinga. Nothing was going to turn me aside. Joy didn't verbalise it, but I'm sure she was hoping for a more sensible compromise.

Taking advantage of the street lights, I got moving at 5:30am. I headed back to the ferry terminal, and turned round there to head for Johnsonville. A couple of friends from the Cavalcade, Stephen and Gareth (see Appendix five) were to meet me in Tawa and guide me through the highways and byways of greater Wellington.

As I came to the place where SH1 turns up the hill, I saw a group of people waiting at a bus stop. They weren't ordinary people but had the unmistakable look of nutters. They were more animated than your normal group of bus waiters, they weren't on phones, they were talking to each other. They were sparkling like the energiser bunny, and they had race packs, and hydration vests with trek poles poking out the top. They were going somewhere they wanted to be. Exercising my journalistic nosiness, I asked one of them:

'Do you have a race on this weekend?'

He connected instantly and smiled the smile of brotherhood. 'Yeah, we've got a 100km ultra tomorrow in Taupo. The race has been cancelled but a few of us are just going to do it anyway.'

'I did the Taupo 100 a couple of years ago. It was great.'

I got instant respect. All four of them gathered round to talk. It wouldn't have mattered if I was an axe murderer, or an embezzler of retired people's funds. I had done the Taupo 100. I didn't even have to prove it, just knowing about it was proof enough. They took one of my new fliers and promised to donate to my cause.

I set off up that hill, and it's quite an honest wee hill, with a spring in my step like I hadn't had for many days. North Island here I come! Joy was there at 'the Johnsonville Shops' as planned. She hadn't been too keen on this whole Wellington thing, but she'd impressed herself, and me, with this outstanding piece of navigation. It was a good sign. We had a coffee break and I headed for Tawa.

On the way I passed the Arohata Women's Prison. Places like this were a big part of my former life, and I had been here several times. The prison was built in 1944 and opened as a borstal for women. In 1987, as a response to the rising number of female prisoners, it was turned into a women's prison. I wondered at the heartbreak those buildings up on the hill above me had seen, and were still seeing.

A bastion of broken families and lives, with incalculable consequences. I continued on, but the spring had gone from my step, and I felt heavy with the weight of crime and punishment. After more than twenty years of trying to make a difference, I wasn't sure that I had.

Joy was already at the agreed meeting place in Tawa, and had met up with Stephen and Gareth. They looked bright-eyed, bushy tailed and ready to go. They were bursting to tell me how best to get through the footpaths and tracks of north Wellington but I didn't care. I just wanted to follow them. I knew if I spent a week researching this area, I still wouldn't know it as well as they did.

The new motorway through Transmission Gully, began at Tawa and the cycleways for that would be great when they were completed, but as with everything about the Transmission Gully project, nothing was finished. The whole business had become a symbol of bureaucratic bungling. The boys knew these footpaths like the backs of their race-hardened hands, and we were soon out through Porirua and onto the coast. We had so much to catch up on and the kilometres just melted away. I had guided them through the Barrier Mountains during the Cavalcade run and now they were guiding me through their wild places. I found the mountains much safer than urban streets. They were runners and walking with me was not their favourite mode of locomotion, but they adjusted quickly and we made good time.

As we passed the Royal New Zealand Police College, we discussed how hard our society is on police officers, and wondered how much of their training time was used in preparing them for the strain that was about to be put on their mental health. When we reached Plimmerton, Joy was there with Geoff, another friend, who was going walk with me to Paekākāriki. Stephen and Gareth bid me farewell and turned back for home. Now they would be able to run, and their eyes gleamed with anticipation as they set off, no longer shackled by the old walker. Geoff had been a friend for many years and had even stayed with us during his University holidays, while shearing sheep in the Owaka district. Shearers are not usually known for being good walkers, or runners, but they are known for grit and determination. They seem to be able to carry on no matter what pain levels or exhaustion are besetting them. And carry

on, Geoff did. 20kms from Plimmerton to Paekākāriki he just kept
striding along. There is a foot path the whole way, on this narrow and
dangerous piece of SH1, that would be by- passed by the Transmission
Gully motorway. When that is opened, this road will become SH59.
Although 40kms from the Wellington CBD, this is usually congested
every morning and evening, for hours. At Paekākāriki we had a coffee
break with Joy and Geoff's wife Katie, then they too disappeared back
to town and their other lives. Geoff had a bit of a Grecian Bend to his
gait, but he'd just walked 20kms without training. Not too bad.

North of Paekākāriki, I took the path through Queen Elizabeth Park,
to Raumati. The park itself was refreshing after a day of Wellington
suburbia. It was sand hills, wetlands and small lakes with birds. Finally
I came out on the expressway cycle and walking path, and followed that
through Paraparaumu. As I walked through the Park, I became aware
that this area had once been a camp for American soldiers during WW2.
This had been Camp Russell. I found a memorial to 10 young Americans
who had perished in the sea off Paekākāriki, during a training exercise
on a stormy June 20th 1943. Like vaccine tragedies, wartime ones are
seldom reported for fear of reducing the effectiveness of the 'greater good'.
Although who gets to choose what is greater, or good, is a mute-point.

The expressway north of Paekākāriki will have a lovely walkway/
cycle track when it is finished but as I progressed northwards this was
punctuated with missing track and bridges. At one stage, after being
turned back by signs of negativity, like 'track closed, go back!', I started
using the expressway itself. There was plenty of room with verges wider
than any I had encountered so far, but it was obviously bad form,
because several people stopped to inform me of my error. One chap in
a Kapiti Coast District Council vehicle, was particularly dark about it.

'Hey, you. This is an expressway, you can't walk on here.' 'Where
would you walk if you were me?'

'There's a walkway just over there, are you blind?'

'My eyes are not improving with age, but they are good enough to
see the sign forbidding me to continue on that track, maybe because
that bridge over there isn't finished.'

'Oh, hadn't noticed that. Nah, you're good.' 'Thanks'

When I finally reached and crossed the Waikanae River, the track disappeared altogether. I had arranged to meet Joy in Waikanae, but hadn't realised the expressway went nowhere near the town centre. The old SH1 went right through the middle of town, where Joy was happily waiting. It had been a big day for both of us, but at least I had a sleep during the previous night. We finally found each other, via a few terse text messages, which would of course, in time, deposit themselves in the trash. We drove out to Waikanae Beach where we found a nice caravan park, with good toilets, and all was close to perfect. We were parked in a proper camping place so we both relaxed. Perfect? No, not really, it was November the 5$^{th}$ and some hardy souls carried on letting off fire-crackers well into the night. I was too foot sore and weary to seek them out and explain to them the error of their ways, so I just lay there and ground my teeth. Each time we were drifting off to sleep, another volley of whooshes and bangs would echo across the bay. I have never really understood why we celebrate Guy Fawkes, anyway. 61kms, in the North Island. We were over half way.

**_Joy Leslie: Things learned on the Great March North:_**

44. *Wellington trafic is unceasing. We drove off the Ferry at 12.30, night, and because Rog wanted to start early, we just pulled into a park by the Khandallah turn off. That, coupled with the late-night coffee, didn't produce many zzzzzz.*
45. *I think I have left my hay fever behind in the South Island.*
46. *Rog has walked his behind fair off, and now needs a cushion for padding when he sits down.*
47. *All those P towns that you hear mentioned on the News, like Porirua, Paekākāriki, Plimmerton and Paraparaumu, are actual places.*
48. *Zohar has his own health and wellness business.*

# Day 21

## Waikanae to Foxton

Lace-up on Day 21, after a good night's sleep, was a happy occasion. I was on the second half. Sometime the previous day I'd passed the half-way mark, and the ferry crossing, always an unsure thing, was behind us. At this stage, the road was open to Tirau. The fireworks warriors of the previous evening had run out of powder around midnight, and my nightly leg spasms usually carried on until then anyway. A part of me wanted to go and find the warriors and make some appropriate sound outside their sleeping place. I always felt a bit superior at 5am. I visited the 'What the World Needs Now is Love Sweet Love' loo, just because I could, and we drove back to the walkway next to the expressway. I had noticed it the evening before as we drove to the beach. Only a couple of kilometres between the two ends of each track section. How could anyone not follow that?

Back on the cycleway I was a box of birds, whatever that is, as I usually am at 6am, and strode out for Otaki. I soon got tired of the constant interruptions to the track's continuity, and went the rest of the way on the road. No-one paid me any mind.

Ōtaki – the place of the staff, perhaps with the idea of a staff standing in the ground – this made me smile as I remembered my Aunt who had used a willow staff to bring the cow in for milking each day. When she went off to nursing, she left the staff there, sticking in the ground. When I visited my grandparents, the staff had become a willow tree, big enough to climb in. So I did. Of course.

Joy met me on her bike as I approached the town. She was growing confident with 'park and ride' and escorted me to where she's parked the camper. We had a well-earned break, and while I was eating my pie, I looked out in the street and there was a familiar face, so familiar in fact I knew it like my own brother. Indeed it was my brother. Ian was on his way to Wellington and looking out for either me or the camper. He had spied the camper and went to work finding where we were. He knew we'd be somewhere with pies. He's not stupid that Ian. We had a good leisurely meal and chat and he warned me that the piece of SH1 north of Ōtaki was the most dangerous in the North Island, with many narrow bridges and sharp corners. He was able to quote numbers of roads deaths per kilometre as being the worst in NZ. He also reiterated his view that I wouldn't get through Auckland and to go round the East Cape Highway instead. This was all very reassuring. Ian was a very well-travelled driver and probably knew as much about these roads as anyone about. He also knew from long experience what a stubborn old git his brother was.

In Ōtaki the Rangiātea Church, the oldest Māori Anglican church in NZ, had been built on the Raukawa Marae. This had been built at the invitation of Te Rauparaha in 1850, but did not meet the approval of a dissident with a box of matches in 1995, and had been burnt to the ground. Since then it has been completely rebuilt, maybe including a sprinkler system. The Kapiti Coast was brimming with the history of the many people groups who had lived here. Even Kapiti Island, which could be seen off the coast, had a rich and interesting history. These days it is a world-famous bird sanctuary, and only limited numbers of people are able to visit each day.

Ian's assessment of the road north of Ōtaki had been a good one. The highway was narrow and many of the bridges incorporated a bend. I noticed with sadness many white crosses on the roadside, mostly by bridges. One bridge had seven crosses from three different accidents. Seven people who started their day with hopes and dreams, that ended in disaster. Hundreds of family members and friends affected for the rest of their lives. I didn't know any of these people, but I do know what it's like to stand by a grave of a child, and wish things had ended differently. I hoped the friends of these families, were offered real support, not alcohol, as succour. An often-repeated road sign here was 'Keep Left – High Crash rate'. I hoped they wouldn't keep too far left because that was where I was walking. I would just be getting my heart-rate down from crossing the last bridge, and there'd be another. More than once, I stepped over the guard-rail and hung on the outside until there was a gap in the traffic. What? Risky, you say? This was as a result of the risk mitigation meetings I was having in my head.

The Horowhenua road authority was big on rubbish mitigation. They had posted many signs imploring travellers to use the bins provided and not the road-side as a tip, with 'marginal' success.

I soon crossed the Ōhau river and although it was windy there, I didn't get blown over, as I had in Marlborough. Soon I was walking through the streets of Levin, where Joy Cowley came from. She wrote many books and often wove the issue of mental health into the pages. She was best known in our house for children's books like 'The Terrible Taniwha of Timberditch.'

We were settling into a pattern, which we found worked best. Joy would travel 10kms from each rest stop, and find a suitable place for the next. Thus, the day was broken up into 6 manageable segments. At the last of these she would walk back to meet me. I started looking for her long before she appeared.

Crossing the Manawatu River was pleasant. The new bridge was probably wide enough to walk across, but I didn't need to. The old bridge was still there as a part of a slightly disorganised cycle trail. In the middle of the old bridge was lying a trailer-load of rubbish. After a quick look through it, I found a few items with a name and address on them. All I can say David, is: 'If you are going to dump your refuse in a public place for someone else to pick up, make sure there are no items with your name and address attached! Even better, don't dump your rubbish in a public place!'

The evening was drawing in when I came into Foxton, but I still had a look around. Drawing my attention first was a set of four godwit sculptures in various flying poses.

The godwits, they say, fly from Alaska each year, and many of them come to the Manawatu Estuary, a round trip of 29,000kms. This put my little walk to Reinga into perspective. I wondered if their wings hurt as much as my feet. I wondered too, if there were weirdos among them that didn't want to fly to Alaska? Some that want to do things differently than the rest. But that's how I'm wired.

Foxton had once boasted over 50 flax mills and this industry had been a big part of the town's early history. There had been a carpet factory here too, which closed in 2008, leaving many in the town without work. Another small industry that had been here was 'Foxton Fizz' and I liked the sound of that. I didn't have much fizz about me at that time of day, but I was happy enough, thinking about the godwits and the fizz. I walked past the Foxton Raceway and found a few golf balls near the Golf Links. I did a few kilometres more and called it a day. At nearly 62kms, it had been a good day. I'd survived the bad bridges. Bring on the expressway extension!

We drove to Himatangi Beach where Joy had booked us into the Motor Camp. Bacon omelette was on the menu, and because we were 'plugged in' we had toast to go with it. Either the Waikanae Firecracker Warriors had moved to Himatangi, or their cousins lived here because as soon as it was dark, we had more volleys of explosions to destroy the calm of night. I heard a woman, telling her dog not to worry, that it would soon stop. But he was unmollified and continued to quiver in terror.

**_Joy Leslie: Things learned on the Great March North:_**

49. *The Exeloos on the Kapiti Coast all play you an instrumental version of 'What the world needs now, is love, sweet love'*

50. *I am getting better - mostly - at choosing good parking spots. This was a great one. Smooth surface, and room for the owners to get out past me. Room to pull right in off the road*

51. *I have finally mastered the getting down and putting back up of my bike with the help of the cute wee step.*

# Day 22

## Foxton to Marton

Lace-up on Day 22 was a relaxed affair. Sleep had come after the fireworks. The morning was clear and looking to be a warm day. It was Sunday, so I planned a shorter day, sort of Sabbath Day's journey, and hoped to get to Marton, just beyond Bulls. I got on the road by 6am and loved the quiet of Sunday morning. SH1 north of Foxton was wide and straight, with ample verge for foot traffic. I started humming to myself:

*With road-side flowers of verdant hue,*
*and grass a greener green,*
*The sky was tinged with sapphire*
*blue of heaven's sweet cuisine*

I came across the Manawatu BloKart Club, where small land yachts were zipping about on the morning breeze. The winds were gentle and light but these multi-coloured craft were reaching amazing speeds as they raced around the track, and beat back into the wind. I stood for some time and marvelled at the concept of so much speed from so little wind. I felt heavy and foot-sore as I watched them. I looked at my Hoka shoes. I thought of how I'd read on the box that Hoka meant 'flying, or gliding, over the earth', and I didn't feel that at all. I was into my third day of flat walking and I yearned for a return to the hills. The flats hurt my feet much more.

Joy picked me up at 9am and we drove to Marton to attend church with friends Robert and Eileen. I was given an opportunity to talk the walk, and share what we were up to. It was nice to be in such a supportive atmosphere. It is said Marton was named after the birthplace of James Cook in Yorkshire.

On our way to lunch, we passed the historic building, Armagh House, that had for over 50 years been the Marton Children's Home. I remembered having a calendar of this house by my bed as a child. My parents had financially supported the home. I remembered asking them why those children didn't have homes of their own? It was a new concept to me. I thought I was doing it pretty tough, and here were kids much worse off than me. Unbelievable.

Robert told of All Blacks Mental Skills Coach and sports psychologist, Gilbert Enoka, having spent time here as a child, and having spoken of this in his autobiography. He had attributed a lot of the mental resilience and drive that got him to the top in his field, to the things he learned from the couple that had managed the place. I thought, there's an entire other world going on parallel to what most of us experience. I was hurting in body, but I could stop any time I wanted to. Many don't have the choice to stop the hurt.

After a lovely lunch, we drove back to SH1 south of Sanson, where I'd left off in the morning. The break had been good for me, but the road was as hard as ever. The day was now really hot and I had to step the hydration up. I stopped in Sanson and traded my roadside coinage for an ice-cream, and this brightened my eyes and seemed to bring Bulls a little closer, without taking a step. Ah, without taking a step. In the end, though, I had to get up and move on.

Soon enough I was approaching the Ōhakea Airfield, and welcomed the pause to read up on the history of the place. The airbase had been opened at the start of WW2 and used as a bomber base and training centre for aircrew. The RNZAF No. 75 Squadron had operated Skyhawks from Ōhakea until the Air Combat Force was disbanded in 2001, and the skies went quiet. The Skyhawks were mothballed, well silicon coated to be precise, and sold or passed on to museums around the country. I once worked along-side some of the crew of No.

75 Squadron, when staff from the Air Force were covering for striking Corrections Officers in Christchurch Men's Prison. These men were proud of their Squadron, and had some very unkind things to say about the government of the day, responsible for the 'Skyhawk debacle'.

Less than a kilometre further on, I came to the Rangitīkei River. The bridge had a footpath. It was safe to cross. There was an observation spot in the very centre and I stood and looked at the waters, as was my habit, and wondered where they had been and what they had seen? I was about to find out as SH1 turned at Bulls and headed up the river. For the next two days I would be following the river to its origins. My translator said Rangitīkei meant 'high heaven', that has a nice ring to it as long as one isn't speaking about aroma.

Across the river was the township of Bulls. No really, it's called Bulls. There was once a general store here, operated by James Bull, and it just went from there. The slogan on SH1 read 'Bulls, a town like no udder.' Naturally, I'm a serious writer and wouldn't allow a pun to sneak into my work, but if I did, you'd see (in the order I saw them), relieve-a-bull (public toilet), cure-a-bull (Medical Centre), read-a-bull (Library), const-a-bull (Police Station), forgive-a-bull (Anglican Church), respect-a-bull (RSA), delect-a-bull (at a café), and of course, at the town hall, soci-a-bull. There were more but I'm sure you get the picture. Personally, I enjoyed that the first park I came to, which had three bull sculptures, was called Walker Park. It was rather a nice touch.

I saw our camper parked on the main street with both left wheels on the pavement, thus overcoming the severe camber of the road. Good problem solving, I thought. It was a welcome break as usual with ice-cream and foot massage, but the report of the camper was not so welcome. It was 'playing up again'. The blue skies of my day turned dark with ominous storm clouds, and I came face to face again with the fragile state of my mental health. It was Sunday and we'd have to see what could be done the next day, assuming we made it back to Marton. There must be auto workshops there.

Suddenly the bounce had gone out of my day. Ten more kilometres to the Marton turn-off, to try and salvage a reason-a-bull day of it. No motivation, body not interested, feet definitely not interested, only the mind still wanting to go on, and the mind was 'playing up again.' Regardless, I made it to the Calico Line before darkness, physical darkness, overcame me. 50.6 kms.

We drove into Marton and camped in a caravan park. There was no toilet. There was a toilet, but it wasn't open. At that time of each day my capacity to walk was reduced to 50 metres, so I got Joy's bike off the rack and cycled to the main centre. There were very nice public loos there, but, wait for it! They were closed between 10.00pm and 8.00am. Toileting in Marton is a daytime exercise. There were nice instructions for finding the 'open all night loos' so I cycled there and found the same *'What the world needs now, is love, sweet love'* music was on offer. I thought that the thing 'there was just too little of' was open loos.

There were no fireworks in Marton.

### Joy Leslie: Things learned on the Great March North:

52.  After staying in free/very economical parking places, we went all out and stayed in a camping ground *WITH A POWER POINT!!!* Last night. Himetangi Beach Holiday Park. Awesome place. Making proper toast seemed like the height of luxury. Great facilities also, by the way, just got a little excited about the toast making

53.  I think my sandals are now oficially beyond being rejuvenated by the insoles. Sandal shopping, here I come.

54.  My singing in church this morning failed to turn the head of anyone, but it still felt good.

# Day 23

## Marton to Utiku

Lace-up on Day 23 was early. I hadn't slept well, as was the normal for nights of impending doom. The morning porridge went a little way towards bringing back my Scottish grit, but the resulting war cry was pathetic and heard only by me. I walked back along the Calico Line to SH1, so Joy could get some more rest and then hopefully find a service centre that would look at the fuel problem in the camper. Joy wasn't happy having this responsibility but I think she saw the crazy light retuning to my eyes, and agreed to have a go.

It was 4kms back to SH1, then I was off, heading for the hills. Not massive hills, you understand, but not flat. I smiled to myself as I thought of Terry Davis the trail running entrepreneur, of Cromwell. During the safety talk and course description of the Ultra Easy, a 100km mountain race with 4km of vertical climbing, he described the 250metre Mt Iron, as 'not a hill at all, just a non-flat bit.' I was in the non-flat bit of SH1 North Island.

Joy turned up about 10am, with the sad news that she'd visited five service centres in Marton and had drawn a blank at all five. Chivalry in Marton was dead. A lady in distress was just a nuisance factor, for which they had no time. My morning coffee was more bitter than usual.

Joy carried on to Hunterville and I set off too. My plan was to have the midday break there. I came upon road works before town. There was just one-way traffic and the line of vehicles awaiting their turn, stretched back a couple of kilometres. I just kept of walking, until I came to the front of the line. Because there was room for me to walk along the outside of the cones with a margin of safety, I just kept going. The lollipop man hadn't seen me coming and I was already past him before he noticed me. He hadn't been briefed on this contingency and I heard him speaking into his radio, which until then had been his symbol of power, but was now a symbol of impotence. I could only hear his end of the conversation.

'A guy just walked past here; I don't know what he's doing.' 'Yeah walking. Bro, he's just walking along the side of the road.' 'You'll have to ask him that yourself.'

And so I passed through. It seemed to be their lunch time and no work was actually going on. The two lads with the signs were the only ones to be seen. The graders and rollers were parked outside the mobile smoko shed. When I arrived at sign man two, he also didn't know what to do, but at least he knew I was coming. He didn't have the where-with-all to stop me because he needed the 'stop' side of his sign to hold the banked-up traffic, he couldn't have it both ways. He called as I went by:

'I don't think you were supposed to do that.' 'What was I supposed to do?'

'I dunno, just not that.'

He seemed to be an authority on what one couldn't do but was sketchy on the details of the allowable. He shouted again at my receding back:

'This is a hazard zone; you've got to report to the office!'

'Where's your hazard signage?'

This question appeared to floor him, and he decided to let it go. The system seemed to be more hap than hazard. A few kms further on I came into Hunterville, where Joy had parked in a nice shady public carpark. Small towns are so much easier to do everything. Park, shop, you name it, it's easier. She had stocked up on groceries, and was as happy as a cook with a full larder. The camper was still 'playing up', but was perhaps not as bad as yesterday. We looked around at the town, with interest. It had never occurred to me that Hunterville was named in honour of the huntaway dog, famous in New Zealand's high country for mustering large mobs of sheep and herds of cows. I had owned several of them myself in another time and place. A good huntaway was worth its weight in gold. I had shorn sheep for many years in Germany and found very few good dogs. The good ones were border collies that worked in complete silence, using only their eyes to control farm animals. When noise was needed, it seemed to be supplied by the shepherds themselves, usually in the form of loud shouting, with variations introduced by thrown objects. A good hunt- a-way in NZ is not allowed, on the pain of death, to bite sheep, but in Germany, this seemed encouraged. The Lärmhund (noise dog) was good for blocking holes in fences and hedges, or digging holes under one's caravan at night. Also handy if you thought a lamb needed a good savaging.

I felt quite happy sitting in the camper, and was reluctant to move. If the camper wasn't moving it couldn't 'play up' or misbehave in any other way. If I didn't walk, my feet wouldn't hurt so much. Seemed an easy fix.

There was no service centre as such in town. Like a lot of small towns, there had been 2 of them but they had sadly closed down. You had to go to Marton for anything serious. Ah yes, Marton.

There was a small motorbike agency there so I wandered in there to see if perchance there might be some old guy that could sniff out a fuel problem in an old Rover V8. No, sorry. You'll need to go to Marton. The young man who gave me this depressing news was a salesman, not a mechanic, but his eyes lit up in recognition and he said:

'I saw you yesterday in Church down at Marton. That's a fantastic thing you are doing. I wish I was coming with you. Where have you walked from today?'

'Marton'

'That's 26kms away.'

'It is indeed.'

The old guy tinkering out the back looked a likely candidate to know something about old motors, but he was a client, not a workman. He did look momentarily interested, but the light faded quickly in his old grey eyes, and he said:

'Nah, I better not start something I can't finish.'

Joy headed off for Mangaweka, hoping to find better mechanical support than either Marton of Hunterville, and I set off too, depressed, and on the verge of tears. I needed a ditty to spur me along. It took me some time to come up with something, but time was something I had plenty of.

*Oh, see the rugged musterer – that strolls the craggy hill*
*The sidelings steep, the waterfalls – above the Hunterville*
*And round his feet, the hunt-a-ways – religious silence*
*keep Awaiting shrill the whistle blast – to clear the face*
*of sheep Merinos are a cunning breed – and sneakily inclined*
*And if you give them half a chance – you'll leave them there, behind*
*But Tyke the mighty hunt-a-way – has seen it all before*
*And barks until the stragglers all – are on the valley floor!*

I continued on my way, still foot sore but happier. I came upon a side road, where a Rural Delivery agent was parked in a red double cab utility, by a row of 14 mailboxes. She was sorting mail into each one. I asked if she was enjoying her day? She replied that she loved this part of her role, and that she saw herself as the connection these people had with the outside world. A world that didn't know, or even care to know, what went on in these lonely outposts in the hills. She said each of these mailboxes represents a whole ecosystem, a living organism of country life. She pointed at a yellow box, eyes shining with the memory, and said, 'those folks don't know me from Adam, but they invited me to their wedding anniversary.' I told her I thought people like her were the conduits that connected the lonely outposts. I told her of the D shackles and said I had three to give away. Which mailboxes should get them?

'That yellow one there, that red one down there, and well, I'd like one too.'

'Would you like the stainless one?'

'I would thanks, yes.' 'It's yours.'

I headed off on my way and felt much the better for the brief conversation. I wondered how often the good feeling that comes from conversing with someone, is passed up?

Joy texted me that she was parked behind the café, and as I'd walked well past the prescribed 10kms, I assumed the Flat Hills Café was my goal. But it wasn't, and a careful search of the parking area was fruitless. She must have been distracted by the constant camper problems and driven right to Mangaweka, 27kms away. Flat Hills Café was nice though, in a lonely outpost sort of way, and of course they had a nice toilet, what a relief. Sarah, one of the staff, asked me what I was up to? She'd seen me walk in off the road, and had probably seen me look around their parking area. When I declared my mission, she raised her voice and told the other customers seated around the room. They shouted me the coffee and carrot cake. For a few moments my feet were forgotten and some tears peeped through.

Back on the road again, the remaining kilometres to Mangaweka seemed lost in the mists of time, well the mists of something, anyway. Joy texted me again, saying there was petrol squirting out on the street. I was already in the sloth of despond, so I didn't reply. One foot in front of the other. One foot in front of the other.

In Mangaweka, the camper was indeed parked behind the first café I came to. There was, as Joy had suggested, a strong smell of petrol, so we called the AA again and arranged a tow truck from Taihape. My brother Ian, said he'd bring his spare car down from Turangi for us to use in the interim, and that he'd return home with the tow truck. He's a good bloke that Ian. This arrangement was much to Joy's relief, and may well have saved a full meltdown on my part. The storm swell of stress had washed over me. I was treading water, and gradually sinking. I was too exhausted, or stupid, to lift up my hand for help. I saw a poster for a 'Fakes & Forgeries Art Exhibition' and I thought, the way I was feeling, I would make a great exhibit. One thing I could still do was walk. So walk I did. I set off up the Mangaweka Hill with a vengeance. I sort of welcomed the pain, and walked faster and faster. I abandoned my normal safety valve of maintaining 6.5 kph. I had expected to see the famous DC-3 in Mangaweka, but I hadn't noticed it. This just seemed another addition to my already bad day. A woman interrupted my thoughts as she drove slowly by and turned around to speak to me. I didn't want to talk to anybody, but I was well brought up and this overrode my first impulse to march resolutely on. When I engaged with her, she spoke with a southern Irish accent, probably Cork:

'I've lost my phone; I think I left it on top of the car. You haven't seen one on the side of the road, have you?' 'Not today, but I'll keep an eye open.' 'Thanks heaps.'

'How will I contact you if I find it?'

'Just give me a call, here I'll give you, my number.'

'Do you have another phone?'

'No, why? Oh, I see. Just find 'Himself' in the contacts and message him.'

'Okay.'

'Are you feeling all right? You look a bit out of sorts.' 'I'm okay, just trying to walk away from my problems.' 'Can I give you ride to somewhere?'

'No thanks.'

She drove slowly off, and I continued on my way, happier. I've always had a soft spot for an Irish accent. I entertained myself wondering what 'himself' was like. When I reached the top of the hill, I moved into second gear and set off down towards Taihape. Ian had said he'd be an hour and I'd reached Utiku by the time I saw him. We set off back to Mangaweka, and as I settled into the car the physical madness of walking that fast at the end of an already long day, made itself felt. I had an attack of cramp for the first time since Bluff.

The tow track had arrived and was preparing to load the ancient vehicle for the second time in a week. Somehow, it didn't seem so bad this time as we now had a vehicle to continue on our way. Jo, Ian's daughter, organised a motel in Taihape, and Ian himself went with the tow truck back to Turangi, where he had a house. He had also arranged a garage to receive and look at the camper. Did I say, he's a good bloke that Ian?

We drove to Taihape, the gumboot capital, and settled into the motel. When I showered, I couldn't bend down to wash my legs or feet, and had to rely on the rinse mode. Then we went out to a restaurant for tea. It had been a long day, but 63kms had been covered, with over 700 metres of vertical.

I slept like a log, a log that is constantly ravaged by spasms of cramp. A log that has vivid dreams of running in races where it is lost all the time.

*Joy Leslie: Things learned on the Great March North:*

55. *I can now get the bike on and off the rack without using the wee stool.*
56. *I learned that Manga means stream. I spent some time in the lovely little town of Mangaweka.*
57. *It was to this lovely town that I called our 2nd tow truck of the journey. Petrol was squirting. FAR too expensive to just pour out on the ground.*
58. *Great to be in whanau territory. Ian to the rescue. Will be driving his car until the wretched camper comes out of rehab.*
59. *AA Plus – I salute you.*

# Day 24

## Utiku to Desert Summit

Lace-up on Day 24 was a difficult affair because I could, only with difficulty, reach my shoes. I'd broken out in a sweat, by the time I had the laces semi-tied. I'd retie them later, when I'd warmed up. I took advantage of having 240v electricity and cooked some toast. Eggs and toast with thick avocado spread on it, is as close to perfect food as a long-distance walker can find. I felt as good as gold. This was a term my father had used to describe 'slightly better than expected'. As I'd lain in the night looking up at the semi-dark ceiling and listening to the big trucks doing their quiet rumble through town, I couldn't imagine even walking 10 metres on SH1 let alone following them up onto the Plateau. I just hoped, as I did every other night, that it would be okay in the morning. Now it was morning and I was physically still a mess but I felt positive. We had a reliable vehicle, so I could concentrate on trying to cover another 60kms. What? 60kms? Ridiculous!

Joy got up at 5:30am and drove me back to Utiku, where I'd finished the previous day. She would then return to Taihape and start her day with calmness and dignity. I think those were the words she used.

Utiku was quiet and picturesque with fog in the river valley. As Joy drove away, the pain in my feet and legs intensified, as if loneliness made it worse. As usual though, once I was moving, things started to improve, and after half an hour I was able to reach my feet and lace-up properly. It took about 90 minutes to walk back to Taihape, although I did waste some time photographing the giant gumboot sculpture.

My feet screamed in agony at the idea of wearing corrugated iron gumboots. I returned to the motel for a second breakfast, a foot massage and a serious lace-up. As I returned to the road, I was humming the Gumboot Song. John Clarke had made Taihape famous with his Fred Dagg persona. Up the road a bit I came to a woolshed with a train mural painted on the wall. I always noticed the woolsheds; I'd spent a fair bit of my life in such buildings. I'd shorn through the transition from converted old houses to the modern affairs of today, with showers, kitchens and toilets. None though, had trains painted on the walls. Go Taihape!

I came upon a big 'Man Up' poster. I read and reflected on their movement, where men 'open up, not harden up'. I thought of the many men I'd met who had not had a good father figure in their lives, and how this had replicated itself from one generation to the next. I quietly applauded the efforts of these guys.

It took me five hours to climb up onto the Plateau at Waiouru. I'd seen many signs of the military, from warnings of live firing, to 4WD ruts straight up hills in a way farmers don't travel. Joy was waiting every 10kms and she was becoming pretty adept at the distances. She had to change her food preparation and supply system too, as she no longer had a mobile kitchen. She shopped more often and concentrated on keeping food and drink cool. I wasn't overly sure how she did it, but each time I drank a cool beverage, I was thankful and felt privileged. In Waiouru we had a late lunch at a quiet pizza joint. I took advantage of the quiet by lying down on a sofa for a serious midday rest, and foot massage. The pizza people didn't seem to mind. While we were there, the dark ominous cloud that had hidden Ruapehu most of the morning, reached out and teemed on Waiouru. It was a gully-washer worthy of the South Island's West Coast. I hoped none of the boys and girls of the defence force were out training or camping in this weather. As I set off again, water was rushing down the gutters, but the rain itself had abated. I wore my fluro coat, because each heavy traffic unit that passed, was accompanied by a swirling maelstrom of water. I would turn my back and let each water spout thrash itself harmlessly against my back.

I planned to walk to the Desert Road Summit, which seemed to be the end of one chapter and the beginning of another. In my fragile mind such things were important. There was the water shed. There, water headed off in different directions and would run to the sea hundreds of kilometres apart. I looked across at Ruapehu, now completely free of cloud. It was spectacular. I had once, a few years earlier, competed in the Ring of Fire ultra marathon. This had started at the Chateau and gone right round the mountain to finish again where it had started. It had taken me 14 hours to walk round this active volcano, and looking at it now from the Desert Road, this looked like quite a herculean task. Once, on Christmas Eve 1953, the crater lake on Ruapehu had burst out, and the lahar from this event had swept away the bridge from the main trunk railway at Tangiwai.

A passer-by Cyril Ellis had tried to warn the engine driver by flashing a torch but the front half of the train could not be stopped from plunging into the swollen river, only 8kms from where I was standing. Ellis and the train's guard had then entered the first surviving carriage, which was teetering on the edge, to help evacuate the passengers. While in the carriage, it too plunged into the river, and these two heroes broke a window and got all but one of the carriage occupants out to safety. One-hundred-and fifty-three people died that night and this remains New Zealand's worst rail disaster. I wondered what I would have done in the same circumstances? Would I be that brave? Probably not. I wondered too if Mr Ellis had nightmares about that one girl, he wasn't able to save.

I came upon a sign telling of the Kaimanawa Horses. I had read up on these wild creatures and something of their spirit made me happy. In the middle of each afternoon, happy thoughts seemed to be in short supply, so I clung like a drowning man to them. As I walked along, my footsteps formed themselves into a marching jingle.

*Oh, run the hills Kaimanawa – pure freedom like the breeze*
*That wafts through mountain tussock land – and giant matai trees*
*With thunder hooves and manes a-toss – and streaming tails behind*
*You gallop where your fancy takes – by bridle not confined*
*Your stables are the sunny slopes – your troughs, the snowmelt streams*
*Your course is on the secret trails – and not the ploughing teams*
*Your muzzle velvet, tests the wind – for danger signs and threat*
*and then you prance so fleet away – in equine minuet.*

As usual, such thoughts got me back on track and the road seemed less hard. I didn't see any horses but I felt them. I knew they were there. I hoped they knew I was a kindred spirit. I reached the summit and photographed the sign. Crikey, 1074 metres. No wonder I was tired. Behind me was the Ruapehu District and ahead Taupo, New Zealand's largest lake. I could see its blue in the distance. I could see steam rising from the geo-thermal areas. I could see Ngauruhoe crowned with a fluff of white, like an old mountain man, dispersing wisdom. "There, you see? That wasn't so hard."

Joy came walking along the road to meet me, as she did most days, and we walked the last couple of kilometres together. 62kms for the day, and, unbelievably I could untie my own shoes. We set off for Ian's batch in Turangi, and as we drove through the tight bends of the Waitakihi Valley, Joy raised a previous anxiety about this famously dangerous piece of highway. Many of our friends and advisors had joined to reinforce her worries. 'Whatever you do, don't walk the Waitakihi Gorge, there's been heaps of crashes there.'

It did me no good to remind her that I had survived the Kapiti Coast bridges and Kaikoura highway. I fobbed her off by suggesting I'd decide in the morning when I saw what the traffic was like. This wasn't over, it was parked. We saw our camper in a car hospital in Turangi. It looked a bit forlorn and sad, and I heard it whimper as we removed some essentials for the next chapter of our journey. The mechanic didn't yet know what the problem was.

It was great to spend an evening with my brother, and many old memories were dredged up and laughed about. Ian was firmly on Joy's side about the road down the Waitakihi Gorge. Democracy is better, they say, than tyranny. But not much.

### *Joy Leslie: Things learned on the Great March North:*

60. *After 3 weeks of driving our ponderous, slightly top heavy, usually friendly but occasionally fuel squirting camper, my attitude to driving has changed. I treat corners with great respect, I get quite heady if I get to 100kph, see big trucks and hope I won't hold them up, and lately, with the fuel issues, I have held my breath as I drive up hills. Today I drove a car instead.*

61. *After 3 weeks I had finally adjusted to the indicator being on the left, so today I consistently flicked the wipers at intersections.*

62. *The squirty fuel thing was caused by the return fuel pipe coming loose. Did not know we had one. Hopefully rehab will be over by tomorrow.*

# Day 25

## Desert Summit to Motutere

Lace-up on Day 25 was a slow business. I'd not slept well; it was hot and we had the window closed against pesky insects. At 4am I gave up and got up. When the blood rushed into my feet, I was hard pressed not to scream out loud. I walked out to the lounge, over a bed of hot coals that had not been there the night before. I took advantage of having the time to cut away the bandaging holding my trashed feet together, and giving them a good soak in Epsom Salts. It was unbelievably wonderful. I sat there with a stupid smile on my face, and tried to ignore the sense of impending doom. I couldn't imagine walking on those tattered lumps of raw meat.

After an hour of that I dried them with excessive care, reapplied the tape and carefully pulled on the socks. Last of all the shoes, the trusty shoes. They had survived 1500 kms on hard unyielding road surface and were still in far better order than the feet. Ian is not a breakfast eater and his pantry reflected that, but I cobbled together a meal from Joy's supplies and a few items pinched from the stuff he had for his grandkids.

Ian appeared and we had an uplifting chat about the old days, and some of the dumb things we had done. We must have done some good things too, but the dumb things came more readily to mind. Finally he worked the conversation round to the gorge road, and suggested I'd be an absolute idiot to walk through there. He said there was a good alternative parallel to the road, called the Tree Trunk Gorge Track. I said I'd have a look at that. It was easier than arguing. I noticed he was developing the same cautious approach to making suggestions as Joy had adopted. They were both turning into cunning manipulators.

I hated to waken Joy, she looked so peaceful, but I wanted to get on the gorge road before the traffic woke up to the new day. As we drove up to the desert summit, the dangerous curves of the gorge were mostly hidden by a heavy fog. I took advantage of the fact the safety manager was half asleep, and convinced her it was safer in the fog because people had to drive slower. And so I set off at 6am into the fog with clear visibility for about 10 metres. I wasn't really sure if the fog was real or only in my mind. Everything seemed surreal, I wondered if I was dying. I can look back on this now and scoff at my melancholy, but I was so far into unknown territory, as far as physical endurance was concerned, that I no longer knew where the border was.

There were beautiful views all around me, but I couldn't see them. I sat on a crash barrier and opened up face-book on my phone. There were hundreds of people supporting me, and it came to me that just because I couldn't see them, didn't mean they weren't there. I set off again, still foot sore, but happily feeling the wet fog on my face, and tuning my ears to sounds of the forest. They were there too, I just needed to focus. Soon I also heard a big truck. It was kilometres away but the sound carried so clearly in the fog, it might have been just round the corner. The truckies were all surprised to see me as I materialised suddenly out of the fog, but they were professional and none ran over me. I became rather slick at sitting on crash barriers and flipping my legs over to the outside, while they passed.

Most acknowledged my efforts with a friendly wave or an air-horn salute. I came to the sign indicating the Tree Trunk Gorge Track, but I hadn't really considered taking that path. Normally I would have been immediately attracted to such an off-road option, but my feet were so painful, the idea of stepping on an unexpected stone or tree root, would have seen me collapsing into a tearful heap and sucking my thumb.

As I wound my way down the twists and turns of the road, I reflected on the quirk of the English language that has the word 'wound' (past participle of to wind) being the same word as 'wound' (to injure). Were these the musing of a crazy man? Probably.

Another memory of the gorge was the number of road cones that had fallen, or been thrown, over the edge of the road. There were hundreds of them. A fortune to made by someone with abseiling skills.

A pilot vehicle for a 'Wide Load' whizzed by, flashing warnings to all and sundry (me), heading up the hill. The driver was so surprised to see me, he didn't appear to know what to do, until the opportunity was lost and the fog swallowed us both. Maybe he convinced himself I hadn't even been real, but after him there was no wide load, or any other load to be seen. In fact, there was no traffic at all for a couple of kilometres, until I came to a bridge on the sharpest corner of the road. There, a team of busy men were measuring the height and width of the bridge, and discussing camber and turning circles. They were speaking English, but otherwise I had no idea what was happening. We were all wearing high-viz and they weren't immediately aware that I wasn't one of them. I think if I'd dropped a few numbers into the conversational potpourri, I could have walked on by without actual communication. Then one of them said:

'Hey, where the hell did you come from?'

'Bluff'

'What? Bluff? Wadda-ya-mean Bluff?'

'You asked where I came from. I've just walked here from Bluff.'

'Well you can't walk here, there's a house coming.'

'Okay, I'll bear that in mind.'

'No you won't. You'll get off the f-ing road, that's what you'll do!'

One of the others said:

'No, seriously mate, you'll need to get off the road, there IS a house coming.'

I just walked off and they didn't know what to do about it. In hindsight I could have been more considerate, but I wasn't myself and I have never cared much for being sworn at. As they had said, there was a house coming, and when I heard the big transporter approaching through the thinning fog, I walked into the roadside forest and watched it pass by. A couple of kilometres further I came on the back-up crew holding back the South-bound traffic, which was waiting in a mixture of impatience and acceptance of the inevitable. I smiled to myself at the irony. One of the most dangerous sections of SH1 for a walker, had been wiped clean of traffic by a house, with its escort of fighter planes.

The back-up boys manning the road block, were not surprised to see me, indeed there was an air of heightened relief in their demeanour. It probably would have ruined their day, if they'd skittled a walker. There can be a lot of paperwork with these incidents. One of them twisted his head and spoke to his shoulder.

'Yeah mate, you were right, he's just turned up.' He nodded to me and I replied:

'Thanks for holding these people here for me, that's quite a freaky bit of road back there.'

'No problem. By the way, why are you doing this, walking the Desert Road in the fog?'

'I'm walking from Bluff to Reinga to raise money for, and awareness of, mental health.

'Bloody good show, well done. The fact you've made it this far, shows you've got what it takes. Did you tell those other guys why you were doing this? They thought you were nuts.'

'No, they didn't ask.'

'The transporter radioed that he hadn't seen you, they were starting to freak out.'

'I walked into the bush to avoid him.'

'Ha. We do lots of training for every eventuality, but we've never met a walker before. First time for everything.'

As I set off past the waiting line of vehicles, some of the drivers smiled and waved, others glared at me, perhaps assuming that I had been the cause of their travel disruption. The first of these, a well-dressed businessman, lowered his passenger window and said:

'Thanks mate, it made my day listening to that radio traffic about you. It was like a good TV serial and was building into an exciting climax, when you just materialised out of the fog.'

'Thanks, have a good day.' 'Oh, it's better already.'

Joy was waiting down the road, backed into a convenient gravel pit. She hadn't been sure whether the house truck would be a good thing or not, and was glad to hear my tale. We don't always think the same things are funny, but we were in accord on this one.

The fog thinned and was burned off by the morning sun. Soon it became the hottest day I had walked through. As I approached the intersection with SH46 at Rangipo, I noted a Big Mack log truck approaching from the North. Tractor and trailer unit were fully loaded with logs, and together made a spectacular sight. There is a slight down-hill part there and he was taking advantage of this to build up speed for the long climb that was in front of him. The shiny stainless exhaust stacks were blowing twin columns of black smoke into the sunny blue sky. When suddenly a sporty 4WD with lots of ostentatious bling, unnecessary lighting and fat tyres materialised from the West. Apparently without looking, the driver swung out onto SH1 directly in front of giant truck. The twin columns of smoke disappeared abruptly, and were replaced by blue smoke and howls of protest from 30 heavy-duty tyres.

The driver tried with desperation, to avoid the inevitable crash and annihilation of the SUV. I too, hoped he would avoid the impact, because I wasn't far enough away to be safe. My legs wanted to run away, but my mind knew it was far too late, and my eyes were fixed on the terrified face of the young man at the wheel of the truck. He was the right driver, in the right place, at the right time, because he managed to bring the juggernaut under control, and another idiot survived, to drive another day. I was acutely aware that I too owed him my life. When things were under control, his terror gave way to anger and this rush of adrenaline was expressed in a long blast of his air-horn. He almost came to a halt, before the smoke from his exhausts reappeared and he drove on.

If he had stopped, I would have gone back and given him a hug, we both needed it. Hundreds of dollars-worth of rubber was smeared in black streaks on the road and filled my nostrils with its acrid stench. 'Those sharp corners on the Desert Road are dangerous,' they said. Ha, the straight parts were far more deadly. I can't remember for sure, but I may have omitted to mention this incident to my health and safety manager at the next refreshment stop.

That young man's face is imprinted in my memory, and if I ever meet him, I'll still give him the hug. My brother Murray drives a log truck and he once told me, not many days go by without someone doing a kamikaze pull-out in front of him. At that moment I had a lot of empathy for him and all the other drivers of big rigs.

As I continued down the valley, I saw evidence and signage that reminded me this area was where the Tongariro Prison Farm was situated. I had visited it a few times in my former life and wondered how the boys were getting on. I wondered how many had mental health issues, which were being exacerbated by the government's ban on visitors to prisons. I suspected many did not care, but I did. Besides the men themselves, their families were getting trashed too.

I'd been in Turangi before but as usual I hadn't stopped to look, to really look. There's nothing like a hurting body to make one pause to smell the roses, and all those other activities enjoyed by the turtles of this world. Turangi was built to house construction workers for the hydro-electric project on the Tongariro River. Now the major employment industry appeared to be the prison.

In Turangi I enjoyed three pleasures not usually available on the road. A pie, an ice-cream and a visit to the toilet. It was hot, easily the hottest day on the trip. We went round to the car hospital to visit our camper, but it was too sick to see us. Parts were on order. There would be no discharge that day, so I set off towards Taupo. As I crossed the road bridge over the Tongariro River, I noticed it had been constructed in the same year as I. There was a footpath across the bridge so somebody had been a visionary back in 1955. There was a sign, assumedly erected since then, prohibiting jumping or diving from the bridge. There was also barbed wire strung along its length, to back up this prohibition. If one insisted on diving into the relatively shallow waters of the Tongariro, one would do so having already been cut to ribbons on the wire.

At the other end there a sign forbidding walking on the bridge, but I was already across, so there was no going back. Perhaps these signs were indicative of Turangi. This road was called the Volcanic Loop Highway, and I did feel a bit loopy walking on it. After a few kms I was walking along the edge of Lake Taupo itself and this brought, apart from the beautiful views, a cooling breeze to settle the heat of the day. I saw pairs of swans with their cute fluffy little cygnets. One pair threatened me and contemplated an attack with aggressive necks outstretched, but they decided to let it go, perhaps sensing I couldn't run away so would stand and fight.

I called it a day at Motutere, making it 61kms for the day. We returned to Ian's place in Turangi and after cleaning up and trying in vain to console my feet, he took us to tea at the home of some Indian friends and we shared a lovely meal with them. It is possible they thought I was a nut job, but they were immaculately polite. As usual when facing with hot curries etc, my bravery far outstrips ability to handle the heat.

I didn't really sleep, but I dreamed and sweated through a continuous series of nightmares. I was wading through hot curries which scalded my feet while massive trucks bore down on me. I tried to run but my burnt feet wouldn't move. Then I would become fully conscious and trucks would be gone, but my scalded feet remained, and I could still smell curry and burning tyres.

### *Joy Leslie: Things learned on the Great March North:*

63. *Automotive workshops are VERY busy. I tried five different workshops in Marton on Monday morning to get them to check out the camper. All were too busy. All Motors Turangi is busy too but he is working on it. Petrol no longer squirting, but still working on other issues. Rehab continues*

64. *Started in the fog on the hill this morning with scary corners. Last 10 kms were along the edge of Lake Taupo – beautiful finish to the day.*

# Day 26

## Motutere to Ātiamuri

Day 26 began as Day 25, in that I didn't really have any meaningful sleep. I was a mess. I needed sleep, I was unbelievably tired, but sleep seemed to be on the far side of a great abyss. I wondered if, after all I had been through, I might yet, not make it. Joy was sleeping but she seemed unsettled too. Maybe she knew more about the log truck incident than I realised. I moved quietly out to the lounge and caught up on my facebook account. Some of my weird supporters were also on-line and this gave me comfort. I wasn't alone in the night. We shared the normal pleasantries of ultra-athletes:

'What are you doing up at 3.00am? Are you nuts?' 'No nuttier than normal, and you?'

'Oh, my mind is never sure whether we're tapering or building.'

'My mind isn't sure whether we've already gone down the plughole, or if we're still at the spinning stage.' 'Looks like you're in a good place then.' 'Have a good day!'

'You too'.

Such an exchange made me feel a little better. A little. Like the captain of a sinking ship seeing a light in the darkness, but still sinking. I rebandaged my feet, goodness knows they needed it, and I had the time.

At 5:30am I laced my unhappy feet into the shoes and walked over the hot coals to the bedroom to get Joy. Seemed cruel to waken her but I needed to be on the road and selfishness is a great companion of self-pity. We drove back to Motutere and I got on the move by 6.00am, leaving Joy snuggling down into the leather to 'finish her sleep'. Fair enough. I needed to get off to an early start because there were some blind corners on SH1 just north of Motutere that I wanted to navigate before the traffic got busy.

This turned out to be a wise precaution as the road round the bluffs wasn't really wide enough for two trucks, let alone some idiot walking there too. Because traffic was light, I could hear the trucks coming and timed my corners accordingly. I wanted to get a photo of a truck negotiating one of these corners so I found a safe spot (well safe-ish anyway) and waited. As anticipated the long vehicle needed the entire width of the road to get round. As I was taking a shot of this, the driver of a car following the truck, stopped to offer me some sage advice:

'Mate! That's a really stupid place to stand.'

I am no great sufferer of fools at the best of times, and this wasn't the best of times, so I replied: 'I suppose the only thing I could that is stupider, is stop my car here, to talk to someone!'

He was not happy at this snub of his community mindedness and replied 'Well f*%^ you then.'

As he attempted to drive off, his huff was slightly spoiled when he missed a gear change, and a loud screech of protest came from his gearbox. I hope his day got better, mine was certainly looking up. Was it Wells that quipped, 'anger is no substitute for dexterity'?

As SH1 left the lake front and headed up the hill, I leaned into the familiar feel of the climb. There were two lanes going up and one coming down. There was a wide verge and a crash barrier on my side. My hypersensitive hearing picked up an unfamiliar sound among the hubbub of traffic. A pinging noise. A freight truck was descending with a loose cargo tie attached to the verge side. The other end of the tie was pinging off the tarmac and snaking into the air like the tail of an angry lion. Its reach engulfed the entire verge, including the barrier. I was not safe, but as I planned an emergency dive over the barrier, the tie came completely loose and flew into the sky like an arrow, trailing the webbing like the tail of a comet. It reached the top of its trajectory and fell again into the middle of the downhill carriageway. I had got no further with my dive than a scared crouch, so stood up again. My body was fizzing with adrenalin but it had nowhere to run. The cargo tie landed just a few metres from where I was standing. My brain, always full of the inconsequential and running now on full turbo, remembered my truck driving brother once telling me, you should never run over a cargo tie. That the hook end can puncture heavy duty tyres and the strap then goes on, to wrap itself around the axel and brake drum, causing thousands of dollars in damage.

Another couple of trucks were descending the hill but were still far enough away for me to dash out on the road and drag the tie safely off. The leading trucky gave me a respectful salute and parp of thanks. You may think an airhorn is a mono-tone instrument without expression, but you would be wrong. You can get a lot of feeling into a toot.

I climbed the hill, enjoying the change of muscle groups if not the foot pain. I met Joy for the day's first rest stop and force feeding. She was getting into the swing of being support girl from the car, with no fridge or gas stove. I wasn't sure how she did it, but the drink was always cold and the food fresh, nutritious and tasty. Soon I was on my way again and enjoying the wide verges of that section of SH1.

I met, for the second time in the last couple of days, a rubbish crew picking up trash from the roadside that people were throwing from their cars. They comprised a warning vehicle, a mule with wheelie- bins and a scissor action arm for grabbing the detritus, and a safety vehicle bringing up the rear. This person was momentarily stopped so I went to talk to her. She said they did this all day, every day. She said they picked up at least 2 tonnes every day. I asked if it affected her mental health, picking up the rubbish of NZ's special brand of slobs? She said:

'I get paid well for doing this, but at the end of the day, I'm picking up other people's shit, and it does get you down!'

I told her of the cargo tie and she said they'd get it, that they pick several up every day. I walked away with mixed emotions, sad for the need of these troopers but glad they were doing it.

I noticed two trucks driving slowing along, and before I reached them, they pulled to a stop. They were linesmen trucks, 4WD with cherry-pickers. From driver seat of the first, a giant bear of a man jumped down, and with a huge grin, he moved to cut me off. He spread his arms wide for a hug. It was Adriaan, who for the last 8 months had been boarding with us in East Taieri. I had known he was doing a few weeks in the central North Island and would be heading home soon, but I had forgotten it would be today. He was looking out for me and was delighted not to have missed me. A hug from such a person was worth a good day of mental health support anytime. We chatted for a few minutes about the road and what it was like walking on the verge of craziness. His crew waited patiently while we talked, and finally he continued on his way Southwards.

Now I could see, and smell, the steam rising from the Wairakei thermal area North of Taupō. The road gently returned to lake level and flattened out. Ian turned up and said he and Jo had arranged for me to go and talk to some school kids in Taupō. This was a pleasant surprise as the Government's bullying of unvaccinated citizens had seen them banned from schools. Soon I was able to leave SH1 and follow the lakeside track right into town. It was an invigorating walk along the well-planned track with the calm lake lapping, and wild fowl frolicking happily to my left, and the traffic out of sight behind buildings or trees, to my right.

When I reached the corner that used to be the centre of town, where SH1 turned away from the lake, Ian and Joy turned up to take me to the school.

Lake Taupō Christian School, turned out the entire senior department to hear what I had to offer. They were well behaved and attentive. I followed the same theme as with the other schools. I asked what one does for a broken leg, and why? They were on the ball.

'You put a cast on it.'

'Why?'

'To give it support while it heals.'

'Good answer – another side question, if you come to school with a cast on your leg, are you a hero or an outcast with the other children?'

'You're a hero, everybody wants to be your friend and people want to write on the cast.'

'Why do they write on the cast?' 'To show support and friendship.'

'Another good answer. Tell me, if someone comes to school with a broken mind, or depressed, or crying a lot, are they a hero or an outcast?'

Long silence.

Finally one brave girl suggests: 'No-one goes near you. You're an outcast.'

'Why do you think that is?'

They all look at each other, embarrassed.

'I suppose because you can't see mental illness, it's not as clearly defined as a leg cast. It's like the dark, we are scared of what we can't see.' This girl will go far.

'Do you think if we can give enough support to the broken mind, it will also heal itself like the leg bone?'

'Yes. Although, I must confess, I've never thought of that.'

'Well I must confess that I and my generation have been very bad at this, but as I look at your young faces, I have greater hope for the future.'

When the session was over, the Principal thanked me and asked that two of the children pray for me. Both the prayers asked that the Lord guide me through Auckland. Amen to that. Auckland was looming as a serious storm cloud on my horizon. It was Red Zoned. No unauthorised movements, in or out. Now the rot had spread to Hamilton and the whole of Western Waikato.

Joy dropped me back in Central Taupō where Jo had arranged an interview with David Beck, a reporter from the *Rotorua Times*. He asked good, well thought out questions and seemed genuinely interested in my mission and efforts. He also asked me, how I intended dealing with the 'traffic lights' in Auckland? I told him I've always been the kind of musician that plays things by ear, rather than following the music. Joy was sitting in the background, and she rolled her eyes theatrically at this. I had walked over 1500kms and this was the first newspaper to show enough interest to send a reporter.

After a bite to eat, I crossed the Waikato River and set off out of town on the old main road. I was watching out for friends Duncan and

Shirley, but there was no sign of them. I found the Wairakei Thermal area very interesting. I loved the idea that you can harness and over-abundance of hot air and generate electricity from it. I briefly considered taking a look at the famous Huka Falls, seeing I was in the area, but my body held a team meeting and the feet vetoed the idea of any steps that weren't directly involved with getting to Reinga.

I reached the round-a-bout with SH1 and set off resolutely up the hill towards Hamilton. After an hour or so, Joy texted me:

'I'm at the Lava Glass Blowing factory, should I wait here until you come, or do you need something first?'

This seemed a mystery, so I googled the 'Lava Glass factory' and found it on SH5 heading towards Rotorua. I texted her back:

'Did you turn left onto SH1 at the Wairakei round-a-bout?'

'Might not have. Sorry, I'll come back. Which way will I turn at the round-a-bout?'

'Turn right, towards Hamilton.'

'I didn't think we were going through Hamilton.'

'We're not, but please turn right anyway.'

She did, and soon she was pulling into a near-by gateway. Normal service and loving support, was resumed. Duncan texted us again:

'Where are you? We can't find you on the Old Main Road.'

It turned out there was another road north of Taupō, called Old Main Road. Soon they turned up too. It had been a great day of meeting cool people. Shirley joined me to walk a few kilometres. Soon she was regretting her choice of sandals as road-walking footwear. She was also spooked by the traffic and how close they whizzed by us. I told her of my learned ability to tell vehicle types by sound alone, and gave her a few sample descriptions. She was suitably impressed. It was great to talk with her and catch up on her life and family.

She was fascinated with the trip so far and could scarcely believe I had walked day after day on this thin strip of verge, with traffic zooming by only centimetres away. Her feet were already sore and she enquired as the condition of mine. I didn't tell her everything but did recount the story of Joy getting the salt water at Kekerengu. We laughed about that, but not the story of the log truck. She looked searchingly at me as if she realised, I only had a tentative hold on stable mental health.

We soon caught up with Duncan and after a refreshment break with them, I set off again, alone. A few kilometres walking with a bubbly, effervescent person like Shirley, made walking alone especially hard. Dark clouds of depression gripped my mind and I shed a tear or two. It had been a long day. I'd met a lot of people and my emotional cupboard was bare. I wanted to reach the Waikato river, but when I reached Ātiamuri, I'd had enough, and happily hopped into the safe haven of Joy's car. She had failed to find accommodation in the immediate area, so we returned to Taupō, and took up Jo's offer of a bed at her place. We filled up the car with the most expensive fuel purchased on the whole trip. Cheers Taupō. 61kms for the day.

It was a good evening with Jo and family. She had been following our travels and had contributed in no small way, with her internet skills.

### *Joy Leslie: Things learned on the Great March North:*

65.  *Sometimes when looking into the distance to see if Rog is getting close, I see a yellow glow and think it's him, only to realise that it is actually an AA sign warning motorists to look out for e.g. pedestrians or ducks.*

66.  *When I visited the lovely Lava Glass studio and cafe, I was actually on the wrong highway - should have turned left at the roundabout.*

67.  *We are hoping to be reunited with the camper tomorrow. Whanau to the rescue for accommodation again tonight. Thanks Jo.*

# Day 27

## Ātiamuri to Putāruru

The new day began about 4.00am after about five hours of comparatively good sleep. Jo's daughter had given up her bed and room to her crazy uncle, and it was mightily appreciated. The bed creaked but sleep was had. Maybe the creaking was good because it was in sync with my body. I tip-toed out to the kitchen and busied myself with the new day. Trying to imagine walking on those feet for another day wasn't easy, but it wasn't new either. The breakfast was a mixture from Jo's bounteous larder and Joy's freshly enhanced supplies. The house hadn't stirred by the time we left at 5:30am.

Back at Ātiamuri, I hopped out and stood on the side of the road with trembling legs and impossibly sore feet. As with all the other days, though, I set off and soon forgot the suffering as the wonders of another new day beckoned me on. I loved the early morning. Traffic was light and I could hear the birds singing.

Before I reached the Waikato River bridge, I noticed a strange dome of volcanic rock standing out from the valley floor, with a monk-like fringe of forest around the base. Research told me it was called the Pohaturoa Lava Dome. Its summit was 245 metres above the river. It had featured prominently in the history of local Iwi, as a vantage point to keep an eye on enemy movements. Legend has it, a Māori chief named Tokoroa was killed in a siege of Pohaturoa. At any other time I may have considered climbing to the top, but not that day.

The bridge over the North Island's biggest river was modern and had a walk/cycle lane. There was no danger, particularly at 6:30am. I stood and looked at the river and wondered what stories it had to tell? I had my own story a few kilometres down-stream. A couple of years previously I'd walked a marathon which ended at the Whakamaru Camp, not that far from where I now stood. It had been a hot day and I had suffered severely from cramp. I had composed a poem about pain, as I limped along, calling it The Taniwha, which was the name of the race, and a monster of Māori legend (see appendix 6). When I reached the finish, I stood for a while in the river until the worst of the symptoms dissipated. Then I sat in my rental car and wrote down all the lines I could recall. If one wants to write about cramp, it's best done while the legs are still twitching.

The triggers of cramp are not fully known, but what is fully known, is that one's fitness must match that of one's pace. On that occasion, it didn't.

The 10km break was taken at The Bull Ring Café. The day was improving in leaps and bounds (figuratively) and I set off again with (almost) a spring in my step.

Tokoroa was the only significant town on my planned route for day 27, and as I approached it, I noticed the shine of gold glinting in the roadside gravel. I took a lot more notice and, in the end, found $15 in one, and two dollar coins. It was my biggest daily haul of the whole trip, and I'm still not sure why it was there. Tokoroa has a reputation (deserved or not) of low socio-economic living, but it seemed some of the inhabitants had money to throw away. I intended to put it to good use.

Long before reaching the town centre, I could smell fish and chips, and I followed it like a shark sensing blood in the water. There was a lot of spectacular sculptures in town and I set about reading and soaking in the history as one might, a hot bath. The sculptures were a mixture of Māori art, Chainsaw wielding men, and Taniwha.

Tokoroa's main claim to fame and jobs seemed to be the Kinleith Pulp and Paper Mill nearby. The town had a friendly feel and I was reluctant to leave. Of course, fish and chips paid for with roadside money are hard to beat.

The countryside north of Tokoroa, was to me, unremarkable. It was dairy land and cows were everywhere, and milk tankers filled the road. I finally came to Fonterra's Milk Powder factory at Litchfield. This was a fairly new plant, and was for a time, the largest milk drying plant in the world. Processing over 4,400,000 litres of milk a day. That's a lot of milk, and a lot of tankers (approx. 160 truck and trailer units per day). Road walkers have a lot of time on their hands, to do sums. Takes their minds off their feet (a bit).

I saw long lines of cows, walking with bovine acceptance, to and from, milksheds and pasture. They seemed to be creatures of habit, and as long as nothing disturbed the habit, were happy with their lot. They were curious about the guy walking along the road, and stopped their walking, if not chewing, to stare.

Joy had arranged accommodation with my cousin Kerry and his wife Merren. In the heart of south Waikato dairy country, it seemed fitting to stay with dairy farmers. Just short of Putāruru, she convinced me we should not be late seeing we had been invited for tea as well. The wording she used were a suggestion, but the tone was not. I hopped, well collapsed painfully, into the car where there was always an awkward minute or two, while I saved the Strava record for the day, and posted it on Facebook. After being alone most of the day, Joy naturally wanted to talk. I'm a typical monofunctional male, and can't deal with two things at once. I'm sure that during these times, many important details fell irretrievably, into the abyss of lost communication.

Kerry and Merren are always fun folks to visit, with a wide interest in people and current events. Kerry is something of a cook, having learned the craft in the RNZAF. We had steak and chips with mushroom sauce. For once I felt like eating. Kerry forecasted rain on the morrow. 'Take your coat!' he said.

Merren quipped: 'He's walked here from Bluff, obviously comfort doesn't register with him!'

It had been a good day, with nearly 64kms knocked off.

### *Joy Leslie: Things learned on the Great March North:*

68. *Retail therapy is a real thing. Had a fun time in Taupō yesterday. Bought some new sandals!*

69. *'It will be ready tomorrow' doesn't always come true when dealing with ageing campers and garages.*

70. *Next suggested release from rehab is Monday. Still driving the car – thanks Ian and still staying with whanau – thanks Kerry and Merren.*

# Day 28

## Putāruru to Tatuanui

Day 28 started refreshingly. I had slept well, perhaps the best sleep in three weeks. The five hours, of the impossible dream, was now within reach. I didn't awaken until 4:30am. Kerry soon joined me and we breakfasted together. It was raining, as predicted. Kerry was happy, it was far too dry. I was not so happy, but the weather had been great. This was the first serious rain since day three in Southland.

Joy dropped me off three kms from Putāruru, where I had finished the previous night. It was the same geographical reference point, but not the same world. Balmy sunshine had been replaced by torrential rain. I put on my fluro rain coat and hopped out into a large roadside puddle. It seemed pointless to try and keep dry feet anyway, or keep anything dry, for that matter.

As Joy drove away, the car was immediately swallowed by the impenetrable wet. She would drive to Tirau, about 14kms away. The rain seemed to enhance my usual melancholy and loneliness. I stayed on the left side, partly because the verge there was wider, but also because the swirling clouds of spray thrown from the wheels of the trucks, seemed less depressing flung against my back, than front. There was no loitering in Putāruru. No reading signs. No soaking up the 'feel' of the place. No finding out what people there did for fun, no researching their history. Pity really, it was probably a nice place on a nice day. I did smile ironically though, as I passed the Big Chill Distribution Centre. I had warmed up and was no longer miserable. I was inward looking and my survival mode was turned up to 'full'.

The swish of wheels had a rhythm to it and my creativity kicked into gear.

*The waves of rain, that fill my brain – a thousand swishing wheels*
*the drenching wet, my feet beset – and down my neck, it feels*
*my undies damp, as on I tramp – with such despondency*
*I search the sky, for signs of dry – in vast hydrology*
*I dream of sun, and Summer fun – and basking on the beach*
*this moist advent, my heart's lament – of things, beyond my reach!*

Years of doing ultra-marathons had made me resilient to trials and discomfort, so I went into a state of torpor like a mountain Rock Wren in winter.

In Tirau we planned to meet Linda and Moira, a couple of hard-case girls we had met during the Twizel Cavalcade. They were driving over from Ōhope in the Bay of Plenty, some 145kms away. That's a dedicated support duo. I would not have been surprised if they had called the whole thing off, and sensibly stayed at home. Also, there was an off-chance Des Williams, editor and friend of Hamilton, could escape the ever-tightening grip of lockdowns that were besetting the upper North Island.

I finally squelched into Tirau, where Joy had found a warm, dry, and open, place in the form of Lola & Co Café. I took off my saturated jacket and left it by the door, but there was no hiding the general state of wetness, that dripped accusingly all about my chair. I was just wrapping my cold fingers around a large flat white, and inhaling its intoxicating aroma, when Linda called to ask where we were? They had arrived, they were girls of purpose, a drop or two of rain didn't dampen their enthusiasm.

Soon they swept noisily into the café, like a breath of fresh might have, into the Black Hole of Calcutta. There was a certain presence about these two, that couldn't be ignored. Soon the room was full of laughter and cheerfulness. Then Des turned up too and it was a party.

Joy later apologised to the staff at Lola & Co for the noise we'd made, but they were glad of it. They said they didn't hear much laughter these days in Tirau and that we had made their day. Several customers had commented positively on the hubbub. Des is the editor of *Shearing* magazine; he's used to noise.

Tirau (a place of cabbage trees) is a sweet little town. A dividing of the ways. SH1, 27 and 28 all meet there. It was once a coach stop for travellers. The information centre is famous in the central North Island for its animal shaped corrugated buildings. The town was once dubbed the 'corrugated capital of the world.' One of the animals appeared to be keeping an eye on the street, with what is known in our house, as a 'side eye'. Almost as if it were saying 'I'm watching you, and I'm not sure I approve of your actions'. There is a gaily painted 'outhouse' with cartoon characters on the walls. I'm always attracted to a good outhouse.

There was a general air of fun about the place. The day had taken a definite turn for the better. Des came with us to get a photo of the girls and me under the Tirau sign, as we set off determinedly on SH27 towards Matamata. Des himself would attempt to break back into the theoretical prison that Auckland and West Waikato had become.

We settled into a congenial 'walk in the wet' pace that suited our differences. Grumpy old man, long legged Moira and shorter but bouncy Linda, soon found a symbiosis that ate up the kilometres.

Laughter makes one much more impervious to rain than a coat.

Then I blundered into a conversational minefield, and heard, too late, the click of a primer under my foot. Blundering and minefields seem to be a personal speciality. They were discussing Ōhope, their hometown and I wanted to show my geographical prowess by asking Linda if, as a paramedic, she had been involved the rescue work after the Whakaari (White Island) eruption some two years earlier? The easy-going banter stopped with a crash and after a long, painful pause, interspersed only by the sound of wet traffic, she said she had been a part of the team receiving injured patients back on the shore.

I glanced at her face and saw deep hurt and tears showing through the laugh-lines and raindrops. I was incensed at my stupidity, but as with anti-personnel mines, it's the stepping off them that causes the most damage. Linda was gracious and said she wanted to talk about it. Not so much about the incident, but the aftermath, the sleepless nights, the recurring nightmares. All three of us cried as we walked and talked over the heavy burden carried by service industry staff and volunteers. Something that many people never give a second thought to.

Then as a distraction, I spied a $2 coin in the wet roadside gravel and we dried our eyes. Metaphorically anyway. We also found a fast-food bag, into which some moron had neatly packed the remnants of his/her meal, before throwing the whole shebang out the window, for someone else to deal with. Moira, ever kind Moira, suggested the $2 coin had be left by the same person by way of recompense. I, ever the cynic, doubted it.

10kms up the road, Joy turned up to take Linda back to her car, while Moira and I splashed on alone. Linda drove to Matamata and then ran back to meet us. By this time Moira, the eagle eye, had found $4 more. She's a scientist and knows how to see things others have missed.

The girls had packed a picnic lunch of scrumptious and nutritious food, but it was no day for a picnic, so we went to McDonalds in Matamata and dripped on their floor while we drank welcome hot beverages. Joy and Linda returned from ordering the drinks with big smiles. They had asked permission to consume our picnic while we drank in their premises? The friendly girl had said we could, then asked Linda if she would be using a gold card for the drink purchase? She had assumed Joy was Linda's mother and was helpfully pointing out, money could be saved. Linda asked: 'How old do you think I am?' The poor girl dissolved into embarrassment and confusion, and tried unsuccessfully to dig herself out of the whole she had created.

Like in Tirau, the noise we created was disproportionate to the size of our small soggy group.

It was very sad for me, and probably Joy too, that the girls had to head back to Ōhope, and take their fun and frivolity with them. I tried to package their good mood and take it with me like left-over food.

But as I splashed out of Matamata, the rain soon drowned all that. I noticed for the first time that the rumble bumps on the side of the road in those parts were shaped like teardrops, thousands of teardrops. And I couldn't help but think of Linda, bouncy, funny Linda, helping horribly injured Whakaari survivors, and giving them succour from the pitifully small arsenal available to her. Knowing all the while that some of them would not survive, and others would live but would carry the scars to their graves. I heard again her heart-wrenching summary: 'Not all scars can be seen.' I thought of the teardrop rumble strip and realised it was another verge on my pathway. Being on the verge of tears.

I found myself singing with the pop group, The Cascades: 'Listen to the rhythm of the falling rain – telling me what life is all about – rain, please tell me, now does that seem fair...?'

I have little memory of the 27kms between Matamata and Tatuanui. Sometime along the way, the rain stopped and I could see the Kaimai Ranges off to my right. Their beauty though, was lost on me. Joy fed me, massaged my feet and tried to keep my spirits up. Without her help, I wouldn't have made it through that day. She saw what a mess I was and had stopped talking about Reinga. She was subtly trying to divert my gaze to more achievable goals. Goals that didn't have a locked down Auckland spread from coast to coast across the path. Ian, whose car we were using and whose advice I greatly valued, was saying the same thing, but the call of Reinga was what was keeping me going. I doubted greatly if I'd last more than a couple of days if I could no longer hear it.

Duncan, who had met us on the Taupo road and with whose cousin Merren we had stayed with the previous night, had arranged for his brother Hamish and sister-in-law Justine to put us up near Morrinsville. They were on a dairy farm there. It appeared Duncan was related to, or friends of, most folks along the road.

Tatuanui seemed like a good stopping point at 62 kms for the day. The town itself didn't amount to much in the big scheme of towns. There was a school, a memorial hall and a clutch of houses. There was a large factory across the paddocks, which turned out to be the Tatuanui Dairy Plant. Joy picked me up at the round-a-bout of the intersection SH27 and SH26, and I melted into the comfortable leather while I did my thing with Strava and Facebook. I wondered if this might be the last entry. The odds seemed stacked higher every day, while my resilience was becoming more and more threadbare and feeble.

Hamish and Justine weren't at home when we arrived, but their daughter Kimberly welcomed us with typical rural NZ flair. She was fascinated with what we were doing, and her encouraging questions did just that, filled me with courage. Perhaps I could carry on after all. One more day anyway. Hamish and Justine, when they came home, were similarly enthusiastic. Dairy farmers know what it is to carry on, regardless of the obstacles. Although a look at suicide rates among such farmers, might give pause to that.

62kms in the wet. Not too bad.

**_Joy Leslie: Things learned on the Great March North:_**

71.  *Rain has been the theme today, and friends joining the walk.*
72.  *North Island geography is becoming more familiar.*
73.  *Some towns have gone to a great deal of trouble to make their public toilets entertaining as well as functional.*
74.  *Tonight's accommodation supplied by whanau of friends. Thanks Shirley and Duncan, Hamish, Justine and Kimberly.*

# Day 29

## Tataunui to Mangatarata

Sunday, 14 November 2021, I gave up trying to sleep at 4:30am and sneaked quietly out to the lounge. I was an expert at this. I noted where the light switches were the night before, and any squeaky hinges, or floors. The established Sunday plan was to walk three hours, go to a church nearby and return to the road at midday. We left the house at 5:30am and I was limping out of Tatuanui by 5:45. I say limping, but that doesn't really describe my locomotion, as both feet were equally trashed.

I just walked really slowly and tried not to put weight on anything. Joy's normal hearty well-wishes had a slight empty ring, to go with her worried look, and perhaps a little bit of desperation. I wasn't far out of town before I started crying again. No special reason, just crying. What a wimp.

As I warmed up, the level of intense pain went down, and I was off. Not crying but clutching bravery about me like a thin blanket. A kaleidoscope of crazy thoughts bounced around inside my frazzled brain. What I would tell my many friends and supporters if I had to admit defeat? I'd have to repay the funds already donated. What about a couple of days off? I was ahead of my planned 40-day schedule. Would I ever get started again if I stopped? Probably not.

At 9.00am, just after crossing the Piako River, Joy picked me up at the Pioneer Reserve carpark. I paused the Strava app, as per usual, and we set off for a church she had chosen in Morrinsville, using the GPS. This route was on a back road through Tahuna. She was strangely quiet and finally overcame an inner turmoil by saying, in a tone she reserved for very serious things:

'I know you don't want to hear this, and you probably won't agree, but I think you should give up on Reinga, and go round the East Cape and back to Wellington that way.'

I don't remember what I said in response, or even if I did. It was a perfectly sensible proposal, but I only registered the 'give up' part. The words thrashed my tired mind like a whip, and I withdrew into my shell like a startled turtle. I was all hard on the outside and a frightened mess in the middle. The last rational neuron in my brain went pop! I knew in my heart she was probably right, but I couldn't process it. I felt wounded. Betrayed.

Church was a meaningless blur to me, other than a kind lady called Alana offering to make copies of our handout flier.

We bought a couple of pies for lunch and went back to the Pioneer Reserve carpark. I said little. The one thing still working was my need of Joy's support, and an intense desire not to say anything stupid. Angry and stupid things swirled around in my head, but remained unsaid. That's my memory of it, anyway.

I pushed the 'resume' button on the Strava app, hopped out of the car, put my phone on the roof, tied my laces, and set off northwards. Up until that day, I had a good pre-walk routine, but stress is no aid of good routine. An hour later, I reached into my bum-bag to check my speed on Strava, but the phone wasn't there. I knew instantly where it was, but I couldn't do anything about it. An unbelievable wave of helplessness washed over me, and dashed me onto the beach of despair, dragging me across the sharp pebbles as it withdrew. Joy would be happily reading her book in the carpark, and would soon drive off to the 10km rendezvous. How could I stop her? I couldn't. I had little choice but to await her appearance. When at last, she drove past with a happy toot, I waved her down, hoping desperately the phone would still be there. Of course it wasn't.

We returned to Pioneer Road, where I hoped the phone might be lying there unharmed in the carpark. It wasn't there either. What a disaster. All the Strava records and photos of the last 29-days were irretrievably lost. To say I was devastated would not really scrape the surface of my inner turmoil. I walked slowly along the road, checking the roadside, mostly because I didn't know what else to do. For once my feet didn't hurt, but they were so heavy I could hardly lift them. A few hundred metres along the road I saw the phone lying there like a lump of roadkill. My spirits briefly soared but it was shattered and useless. The screen was cracked in a star shaped mockery. One of my credit cards was also missing, and I had a brief search for it, but my heart wasn't in it. I didn't care any more.

I collapsed into the grass and gave up.

Joy came along and suggested we return to Morrinsville to see if a new phone could be purchased. Normally, damage control and problem solving are my business in our relationship, but this wasn't a normal day.

In the electronics department of the Warehouse in Morrinsville, they not only had a replacement phone, but something even better. A really helpful sales assistant. I can't remember her name, and I usually would, but like the log-truck driver of Tūrangi, I owed her a hug. She summed up these customers with a friendly smile. There was a frightened woman who wasn't sure if her best friend and companion of over 43 years would get through the current crisis that he had created for himself. And there was the man himself, who just stared blankly out of crazy eyes. She handled this like it was a common occurrence, perhaps it was. She helped us set up the new phone, transfer the SIM card and get the whole turnout running. The photos were lost, of course, and probably the Strava record, but we might be able to find someone who could retrieve those as well. She re-installed Strava as if this was the kind of thing, she did every day. Well done that girl!

Back on the road again, things were better, but not much better. The business of the East Cape still hung over us like the sword of destruction, waiting to fall and cut us to pieces. I didn't know what I would do. The one thing that was still working was my legs and so I walked, numb and shattered, but moving. The one enduring memory, that penetrated the mists of agony that afternoon, was the raucous cry of wild peacocks in the hills. It reminded me of my parents, who kept a few of these beautiful but noisy birds at their home in Owaka. No doubt to the great delight of their neighbours.

I reached the round-a-bout meeting of SH2 at Mangatarata and Joy was waiting there with the news she had booked accommodation at Pūkorokoro / Miranda Holiday Park. This was situated on the Firth of Thames, nicely neutral between the road to Reinga and the road to East Cape. We hadn't stayed in paid accommodation since Taihape, and although Joy loved the support we had received, she also liked a bit of autonomy, and so she was happy. And because she was happy, I was too.

There were hot springs there and I certainly needed some spring, so soaked away some of my melancholy. I then read up on the history of the place and found my worries weren't so bad. The local iwi, Ngāti Pāoa, had a settlement here called Pūkorokoro and though they were loyal and on friendly terms with the British, in 1863 the frigate HMS Miranda had shelled the village, killing many villagers. They had then set up a fort there and named it after the ship. It looked as if local Māori and I had in common that bureaucrats in far-away places can make things difficult for people going about their rightful business.

Of course, my problems could be solved by running up the white flag, but for the Māori it wasn't quite so simple. They were rightfully upset by the naming of the area after a ship that had shelled a friendly village, but agreement was reached, after asking for 158 years, that the name Pūkorokoro be reinstated.

After a good soak and a calming of the soul, I floated the proposal that there was nothing to be lost by continuing to Auckland. If the road block was impassable then so be it. But if we didn't try, we wouldn't know. I went to sleep, dreaming of approaching the police road block and being shelled by the frigate *HMS Miranda*. I had very realistic dreams at such times and I could smell the gun-smoke.

**Joy Leslie: *Things learned on the Great March North:***

75.   *Roof of the car – not a good place to file the phone.*
76.   *Morrinsville Warehouse has a very helpful girl on the telephone counter.*
77.   *Roadside creeper of the north is honeysuckle – so much nicer than the convolvulus of the south, especially when the sun shines on it and makes it smell good.*
78.   *Snails gather for a siesta/ conference after rain.*
79.   *Giving the lovely friends and whanau a break tonight. Staying in a unit at a camping ground.*

# Day 30

## Mangatarata to Mangatāwhiri
## Mangatarata to Waihou River

Day 30 started with the electric feel of thunderstorms. Just in my mind, you understand? The day was sunny and clear, but this was the big test that had been hanging over the whole enterprise from day one. We went back to Mangatarata and at 6.00am I was off on SH2 for Auckland. Joy headed back to her hot pools, washing machines and heat-pump, for a few more hours. And why not?

Thinking it would be a short day, whatever happened, I set off at a brisk pace. No more keeping to 6.5 kph, I felt fearless and unstoppable. A few kilometres along the road I came to a large roadway information sign, with the chilling words:

'Have your paperwork and Proof of Covid 19 test, ready for inspection at the border!'

Well that was pretty clear, but I was committed so I barrelled on. It didn't say 'a negative covid test' just that one had to have proof of having had one. The road was extremely busy, but mainly with trucks and other heavy traffic. Private cars were conspicuous by their absence.

I reached Maramarua at the same time as Joy caught up. She had seen the sign about covid tests and no doubt wanted to flee to the East Cape, but she must have decided to humour me. We had a coffee in town and the barista confirmed that no-one but essential trucks were getting past the border into Auckland. They were being very strict about it. Some people had been arrested for trying to get past. Joy called Ian, and he, with the help of Jo, researched testing places and discovered we could get one done the next morning at 9.00am in Ngatea, some 10kms to the East of Mangatarata.

A sign at the Maramarua School took my attention: In the middle of every difficulty lies opportunity. Aim High!

It was a shot in my quivering arm. It stiffened my spine and I marched on towards the infamous Checkpoint Charlie of the North Waikato. This reference to Checkpoint Charlie had come from a truck driver I'd been chatting to in the hot pool. He'd said it was just the same as the real thing, freedom on one side and oppressive restriction on the other. It was ironic that the Maramarua School which displayed the sign of lofty ideals and philosophy, was empty of all noticeable life. The normal hubbub of children was locked behind the closed doors of local houses. The carpark was devoid of vehicles. It was a ghost school.

I saw on my newsfeed that North Auckland had been released from Red Zone lockdown and a vague plan started forming in my mind. Perhaps if I could get past Auckland, I could continue on my merry way. 'Merry' being a strange word to describe pain and tears. The roadblock was rumoured to be at Mercer, but I wasn't sure of this. My phone map suggested SH2 didn't even go through Mercer.

I discovered the police roadblock at Mangatāwhiri. I saw it from afar, as I was looking out for it. This had been the focus of several hours of walking. It seemed to be teeming with blue uniforms and a line of trucks stretching back a kilometre. There was also a shorter line of cars being dealt with separately. I didn't see any of these proceed through the checkpoint. Some turned back after a brief exchange, while others, after a lengthy period of discussion and paper waving, turned back too. Most looked angry, but a few were philosophically shaking their heads. One kindly looking old man, shouted as he drove by: 'You're wasting your time mate, nobody's getting through!'

I got a lot of strange looks from these rejected drivers. I suppose they wondered what this idiot was doing walking along the road to nowhere?

The road info sign was repeated here. No proof of test, no go!

There was no *HMS Miranda* shelling the roadblock, but I wondered if I did smell gunpowder in the faint breeze. I recorded the 30km morning walk and turned back East. I returned to Maramarua, completing 16kms, as part one of a plan to put 60kms in the theoretical bank of road walking. I guessed 60kms would be enough to cover the section I would miss by driving through Auckland, instead of walking. As a part of this sketchy plan, we would get a covid test at the Med Centre in Ngatea, when it opened at 9.00am the next morning.

Joy then drove me back to Mangatarata, where I set off eastwards through Ngatea to the Waihou River on SH2. This was another 14kms, making 60kms for the day. Thirty on the Bluff to Reinga path, and 30 in the bank. Joy had found motel accommodation in Ngatea. While I showered and treated my feet, she went off to get some food.

'Theres some chicken and chips advertised along the road, are you happy with that?'

I was happy with anything. I really didn't get hungry anymore, and ate only because I knew I should. I was still apologising to my feet, when she returned with pizza. 'Chicken and chips' were shut, boo on them. The pizza was good. I dozed, as I usually did, waiting for the leg spasms and twitching to abate enough for proper sleep. I wondered vaguely where we'd be the next night? Tauranga? Orewa? The trail was spinning out of control. I dreamed of Joy crashing the checkpoint, and us both running away with bullets whizzing about our heads. Even when I was awake, the line between reality and the bizarre was thin indeed.

### *Joy Leslie: Things learned on the Great March North:*

80. *When you are moving on every day and seeing new people, it doesn't matter that you only have 2 sets of clothes. the rest of our stuff is in the garage in Turangi.*

81. *New World is a nation-wide company, but there have been quite different responses to Covid as we've travelled around. Still not taking bags in in Turangi, very particular about queueing in Tokoroa.*

# Day 31

## Waihou River to Karangahake Gorge
## Te Hana to Brynderwyn Corner

Day 31, the crunch day. Joy drove me back to the Waihou River and it was still dark as I set off along the road. I wore my highly visible jacket to warn the sparse traffic of my presence. I planned to walk 30kms in the direction of Tauranga, get the test, and return to the checkpoint, with the proof. If it was a 'shake of the head, no go' I'd have the option of having a complete melt-down, or returning to the Karangahake Gorge, with 30kms already up my sleeve, and continue eastwards like any sensible person would have.

It was a beautiful morning and I felt full of confidence. Birds were singing, and water fowl were splashing happily. The bridges were wide enough to allow foot traffic without the usual danger to life and limb. I was determined to enjoy the day regardless what the outcome was. I remembered the two teenagers in Taupo praying that 'the Lord would help me get through Auckland'.

This was the Hauraki Plains. I couldn't really concentrate on it because my mind was elsewhere, but I finally arrived in Paeroa, without getting run over. This was the town of the famous drink, and indeed, there was a bottled statue to commemorate that.

I continued on to the Karangahake Gorge, through which ran the Ohinemuri River. There was road-works on the approach to the gorge, and I got into conversation with a stop-go girl. She was somewhat surprised at my presence:

'Where are you heading mate?'

'Oh, I'm not sure, either Tauranga or Orewa.'

'Orewa? That's north of Auckland.' 'True.'

'You can't go there, it's all locked down. I've heard of people with legit cases being turned away.'

'Yeah, well I'm going to have a go. At least I won't die wondering.'

'Well if you keep walking this way, you'll die from getting run over. Do you know how narrow and dangerous the gorge road is?'

'Not yet, but I'm pretty nippy.'

'My advice is, turn round and go back where you came from.'

I did turn round. I didn't tell her that I'd planned to, anyway. If I returned to Paeroa, I'd have the 60kms I reckoned I'd need to bypass Auckland. As I walked away, I looked back and she was staring after me as if I was nuts, but not as nuts as someone who would attempt to walk through 'the gorge'.

Back in Paeroa I met Joy and we headed back to the Ngatea Medical Centre. We arrived in time to be first in the queue. No-one was to get out of the car. The nurse would come out and collect the nasal sample where we sat. She was a very nice nurse, Susan, I think, and she was dressed to the nines in theatre gown, gloves, and full-face protection. She even had theatre over-shoes. She took the nasal swabs without the usual pain associated with these tests. She didn't try to get 200mm of swab shaft into my head. She asked what we needed the proof for and when we showed her our flier, she went on to give some very good advice.

'Treat those poor bastards at the border with kindness. They've been there for weeks and they're over it. They're certainly over people being rude to them. If you explain what you are doing, and show your flier and this certificate (of covid test proof) they may just let you through, who knows? You'll have to promise to drive right through Auckland without stopping, though.'

We thanked her for her advice, and gentle testing technique. The world needs more Susans.

I drove to Mangatāwhiri, because Joy was nervous and suddenly wondering about the wisdom of it all. We joined the car queue, and inched our way to the front. As we waited, we added our own prayers to the petitions from Taupō. As with the previous day, almost no-one was getting through. The car immediately ahead of us did, though. They didn't even need to show any paperwork. They seemed to be known to the police, and just drove by without stopping. This brought us to the firing line before we were properly prepared, but there was no backing out now. While one friendly young policeman came to my window, another took a photo of the front of the car. Now we were on record.

'Hello sir and madam, where are you heading today?' The million-dollar question.

'Well, I've walked from Bluff and am hoping to make it right to Cape Reinga. We're hoping you kind folk will let us drive to the other side of Auckland, where I can continue my crusade.'

'Do you have proof of a covid test in the last 72hrs?'

'Yes.'

I handed him the all-important certificates and a copy of our flier. He only glanced at the certificates, but he seemed fascinated with the flier.

'How long has it taken you so far?'

'This is day 31, I'm hoping to do it in 40 days.'

'Walking? Aren't your legs buggered? That's only nine more days. You can walk to Reinga from here in nine days?'

'Yes, I hope so, I've been walking 60kms each day. My legs are okay but my feet are a bit munted'

'60kms? Mate, I don't walk 60 metres unless I have to. What kind of support team have you got?'

I nodded at Joy.

'Joy here is the driver, logistics technician, first-aider, cook, bottle-washer, and most importantly, foot massager.' He bent down and looked at her consideringly.

'What's it been like for you, supporting a fruit loop like this?'

She didn't say what it was like, but deep in her eyes there was dawning, a faint glint of hope. She was starting to believe it just might happen. He continued:

'Look, as far as I'm concerned you can go through, but I have to okay it with my Sarg, first.'

And off he went to see the Sarg, taking the flier with him. We watched as he convinced the Sarg. He looked tired and completely over this checkpoint stuff, but his hard, implacable look slowly softened as the enthusiastic young officer told our story. Finally they both came over and delivered the decision:

'Hi, the constable here, tells me you're walking to Reinga, to raise money and support for Mental Health. I'd have to say I'm bloody impressed. This is the best good-news story I've heard in quite a while. So here's the deal. You'll need to drive directly, using highway 2 and highway 1, to Te Hana, that's where the northern border is, without stopping anywhere. Do you think you can do that? You've got enough fuel?'

'Yes, we have enough fuel, and we can do that, no worries.'

'They will know at Te Hana that you're on the way, and roughly when to expect you, so you shouldn't have any problems. It should take you an hour and a half to two hours.'

'Thank-you very much.'

Off we drove. Through the double line of cones, and envious stares of other want-to-be motorists. Soon we joined the trucks, on our way to the fabled city of Auckland. I looked at Joy, and although her hands were still shaking, her eyes were shining.

'WE DID IT, THEY LET US THROUGH! Praise the Lord!'

I was thinking about the proposed two hours. How could it take two hours to drive on a mostly empty motorway, to the northern border? I didn't care though, we were through. Now the road to Reinga was open. Suddenly my feet weren't sore and the accumulated depression of the last few days, blew away like smog on a windy day. I could breathe again. I felt an enormous weight lift from my over-burdened mind.

As we changed onto SH1 at Bombay, we joined hands, and energy flowed between us in the way it had right back at the beginning of, what she was calling, the Great March North (GMN). She was also happy that she now didn't have to navigate the old road through Auckland. She visibly relaxed as we sped past suburb names like Takanini, Manurewa and Manukau. For once SH1 was our friend. My 60kms of accumulated road distance, was nowhere near enough. 145kms were on the odometer when we finally reached Te Hana.

We did, though, commit one little trespass on the way. We stopped before the border! There was the inevitable road-works near Warkworth, and as we stopped, Joy was able to scuttle round to the boot to get some food and drink. When we'd packed the car, we hadn't thought past the checkpoint. That would have been like an East Berliner planning an afternoon picnic in West Berlin, pre-1989. Interestingly enough, I wasn't the only one who had made this comparison.

At Te Hana, as promised, we were expected. A similar photo was taken of the front of the car. This time, there was no mucking about with the rank and file. The Sarg, herself came to the window.

'Mr Leslie, I presume. We've been expecting you. Do you have a spare flier, that we could have? We think this walk you are doing is absolutely fantastic, and we've been a bit short of things fantastic, round here lately.'

She shook my hand, and we were flagged through. As soon as we cleared the lane cones, I stopped. Joy looked alarmed, and asked:

'What are you doing?'

'I'm getting out to walk.'

'Not here!' She was still thinking they might change their minds and come after us with a Light Armoured Vehicle, complete with machine- gun.

'I've come here to walk, and walk is what I'm going to do.'

I particularly wanted to do it in sight of the police roadblock. There was no book-reading or sleeping, for Joy. She immediately accelerated past me and disappeared into Northland, which had been until now, a seemingly impossible dream. Now that we were past the great hurdle of Auckland, there was no point in hoping the camper might be repaired in time to contribute further to the trip. The car would be fine, we had learned to utilise its advantages and minimise its disadvantages. I no longer had the added stress and worry of breakdowns, or the stress of Joy worrying about them, if you follow me.

I crossed the Hakaru River and came into some quite nice forestry areas. The day was nice and the smells were enchanting. I think when I was stressed, the ability to smell, or notice smells, was gone. Now I was at one with the countryside, and again talking to livestock I met along the way.

One group of young heifers decided to canter along with me and maintain the camaraderie. As they approached the corner of their paddock, and therefore the end of their run-zone, they panicked and ran into the fence. There was a pile-up and a scream of tortured wire, pulling through staples. Those which could, galloped off leaving pandemonium behind them. The pile by the fence finally sorted itself into some form of order, and they trotted away looking sheepish.

Can a bovine animal look sheepish? It seemed so. Unfortunately, two fence posts were broken and three of the heifers had ended up on the wrong side of the fence. They were not happy with this state of affairs, but there was little I could do about it. No doubt the farmer would come along and ask himself, how the fence got smashed up like that, and how those three were in the next field? There would be no- one there to tell him. These things just happen.

Joy was waiting at the Caltex Service Station/Shop in Kaiwaka,

which I assumed meant 'food in a canoe' or 'canoe food'. Outside the shop was a sign, offering 'Penguin Fish Bait'. My mind boggled at the idea of slicing up a penguin for a bit of fish food. Joy had told the shop assistant of our grand quest and she had offered some free food and a drink. This was gratefully accepted. She then went on to say the Brynderwyn Hills were far too dangerous for foot traffic, and that I should probably go via Maungaturoto and the old main road. I thanked her, and said I'd definitely consider that option.

I had no intention of going that way, but she had just given me free stuff and it kept Joy off my back for a few more kilometres. Kaiwaka was quite a pretty little town and I was liking the friendliness of the locals. I stopped to talk to several as I meandered through. One theme that came to the fore very quickly, was their contempt for the government in general and the Prime Minister in particular. While the PM wasn't on my Christmas Card list either, I started to feel a bit sorry for her.

I set off again for Brynderwyn, that dangerous hill, and 10kms later I arrived. Joy was parked in the carpark of the old corner service station, at the intersection of SH1 and SH12. She looked as relaxed as I'd seen her for weeks. We drove to Waipu Cove, a picturesque little seaside settlement north of the Brynderwyns, where SH 1 met the Pacific again. I'd booked a cabin at the Holiday Park and it was just the ticket. My new plan, hatched in the comfort of the cabin, was to walk from Waipu, down the coast for 30kms, and then return.

This would give me 60 more kms, and leave just 25kms for the following day, to compensate for the 145 missed Auckland kilometres. I limped along to the office and booked another night.

The previous night we had slept in Ngatea, 230kms away. We had gone to sleep, not knowing where we would be sleeping this night. We didn't know if our whole enterprise was about to come crashing down around our ears. What a difference a day makes.

**_Joy Leslie: Things learned on the Great March North:_**

82. *Covid testing makes your eyes water. We have been tested today as a prerequisite for crossing the border.*
83. *I am back where beaches are as they should be. Waipu Cove salute you. Gorgeous place and we are here for TWO NIGHTS!!*
84. *One of the things I wasn't looking forward to, driving myself through Auckland to be exact, didn't happen. We were allowed thru if we didn't stop on the 145kms way, so Rog drove. He has some kms to make up, but he'll deal to most of them tomorrow. Sorry lovely nieces - Angie, Naomi and Raylee - catch you another time.*
85. *Memories of last time we stayed here visiting Uncle Gordon and Auntie Joan in 1979.*

# Day 32

## Waipu Cove to Hakaru and return

Day 32, up with the larks and sea birds. Actually, I was up after the gulls, and before the larks. I didn't need to get a ride anywhere, so Joy could get up when she felt like it. I'd promised her the night before I would be okay until mid-morning, so she could have a relaxing start to her day. These last days had been stressful for her too, so she was genuinely happy to take it easy. I packed my race pack with water and food enough for 4 hrs, and off I went. The simple plan was to walk south for 30kms and return, making up 60 of the remaining 85kms I still had to complete to compensate for the 145kms missed while following police instructions not to stop in Auckland.

The early morning, once I had limped the burning pain from my feet, was always my favourite time. There was minimal traffic, and those who drove by were mostly professional drivers. They showed me respect and usually waved, tooted, or both. The odd one even shouted encouragement. The road meandered along the coast and the sea murmured encouragingly to my left, as I strode. Mostly there was a walking track adjacent to the Cove Rd, so I didn't need to worry about vehicles.

In fact I didn't need to worry about anything. This was starting out as the most worry-free day on the trip. My feet hurt, but I'd learned to live with that. The dark cloud of depression that had cramped my mind a few days ago, was nowhere to be seen. Our camper was on the other side of the great divide, in another world. Ian's car was going just fine, and Joy had adapted, seemingly without effort, to providing meals and support out of the boot, chilly-bin and glove box. She was still buzzing about not having to negotiate the Great South and Great North Roads of Auckland. The only worry she voiced was the threat of roadblocks by local Māori, upset at government restrictions and treatment of Northland over the last few months. These had been manned up until a few days ago and loomed large on Joy's horizon, but not mine. Cove Rd went over a small hill and descended into Ding Bay and Langs Beach, and while idling along this idyllic shoreline, the sun rose over the Hen and Chicken Islands off in the distance.

This island group had been so named by James Cook in the 18th Century. I was still amazed at how little one can view the sea from SH1 in New Zealand. Of course this wasn't SH1, in fact it wasn't a highway at all. SH1 wasn't far away though and occasionally I could hear the sound of traffic filtering through from the Brynderwyn Hills, a few kilometres away.

I came up behind a seasoned citizen, out walking his little Jack Russell terrier. The dog noticed me first, and gave voice to his feelings, at being surprised. I think he was a bit embarrassed at not hearing me coming. He felt the need to compensate for this neglect, of what he plainly felt was his job. We exchanged pleasantries and the normal 'early in the morning' chatter. There's a sameness about people out walking at 6am. He said he'd lived here all 80 years of his life, and had seen a few changes.

He waved an inclusive arm at the housing, and said this had once been a cheap place to live, but was now a place rich folks were building. They were bringing their 'high and mighty' ways and flash cars. There was a vast difference between the old cottages and the new architecturally designed structures that were perched proudly on every sea view site. Several of these were still in the construction stage. The old man looked at these with contempt, and finally asked:

'What are you doing walking along here, frightening my dog?' This was accompanied with a humorous chuckle.

'Oh I'm on my way to Cape Reinga, from Bluff, in the interests of Mental Health. Walking the whole way.'

Pointing back the way we had come, he said:

'You know Reinga is that way, eh?'

'Yes, I'm making up some kilometres, lost when I had to skip Auckland. Yesterday.'

'You got through Auckland? Yesterday?' 'Yes.'

'Did you go rural? They say that's how you do it.'

'No, I got permission from the authorities.'

'Well don't tell anybody round here about that, we've been cut off for weeks and can't go anywhere. People are a bit over it.'

'They must have thought I was a special case.'

'Well if you've walked here from Bluff, you probably are a special case.' Another chuckle. I liked this old guy. As I bid him farewell and picked up the pace again, he called after me:

'Don't get run over by those rich bastards from Whangarei in their electric cars!'

'I won't, thanks.'

The Cove road then left the coast and headed up into the hills, which I assumed were the seaward end of the Brynderwyns. This would be the Mangawhai Heads. The road wound upward, with hairpin bends and steep inclines. About 7am the traffic became trades personnel, wearing high viz clothing, driving utes and pulling trailers.

There wasn't a single electric car amongst them. Assumedly such drivers went to work at a more civilised hour. When I reached the summit, I sat down at the lookout and basked in the morning sun and fantastic view. I also basked in the feeling of having climbed much higher than I'd realised. This was no mole hill.

The road then descended into the Mangawhai coastal area in much the same way it had climbed out of Langs Beach. Abruptly. I came out of the bush on the flat, and soon turned sharp left into Mangawhai Heads Rd. This seemed to be the main road through the area, and if I persisted, I could make my way back to Kaiwaka, and perhaps greet the Caltex Lady there again.

Along the way, I came to a bus stop, at which was gathered a large group of children. They were characteristic of any such group you'd find in the country. There were big ones bullying the little ones, who were trying to remain inconspicuous, and wait far enough away to avoid the bullying, but close enough to dash back when the bus came. There were gaggles of girls anxiously checking their social media, while flicking loose strands of hair out of their eyes. There were mothers dropping carloads of children off, while others were walking up in various states of readiness and undress. Some obviously hadn't been subjected to any maternal inspection at all.

One car-mother came back, holding a lunch container out to a reluctant girl. She detached from her group and flounced over to take it. She was probably glad to have it, but not glad of the embarrassment in front of her friends, or her mother expecting acknowledgment. I was enjoying the whole show, including the mounting air of expectation as bus time drew near. My own children had grown up when we lived on the Owaka Valley Road. The bus stopped right outside. The kids could leave things right up till the last minute, and they usually did.

The school bus on Mangawhai Heads Road, arrived. It was a big bus, but it needed to be. The seemingly endless stream of children somehow managed to embark in a reasonably orderly fashion. The bus purred away with its precious cargo, leaving the road strangely empty and quiet. There were only a few empty muesli wrappers to show the kids had been there at all. I was able to pick these up because it was early in the day, and I could still bend over.

I then turned onto Molesworth Drive and headed South once more. Joy rang to enquire where I was, and I said I was just passing Oasis Bar and Eatery, so I'd drop in there and order her a flat white. She looked wonderfully relaxed, when she came. I probably did myself. It was a day to relieve a lot of pent-up anxiety and stress.

I had covered 20kms and asked her to meet me with some drink at midday. This would be another 10kms toward Kaiwaka. She said she had noticed a museum in town and would go there and have a look. She's a museum girl, is Joy. Reads all the displays right through. Sometimes to the frustration of others in her party. I found an information billboard that said Mangawhai was named for the stingray that frequented the harbour. As the road threaded along the edge of the harbour, there was a lovely little walkway among the trees, with beautiful views out across the water. I stopped to read of the Fairy Tern, or Tara-iti, which is New Zealand's rarest bird, with only around 30 individuals left in the wild. This was new to me, being a southerner, but I was immediately attracted to their plight, being something of an underdog supporter. Or under-bird supporter perhaps?

I took another sharp corner and was then on the Mangawhai Kaiwaka Rd heading out of town. On the side of the road, among the normal flotsam, was a stuffed rabbit. This was a loved rabbit, not the normal roadside critter, assumedly thrown out the window by a small child, who was even now decrying its loss. I put it in a prominent position where it could be easily found, or recycled, whichever came first.

Further along, I passed a home among the trees, and out of the gateless driveway exploded four noisy dogs. They chased after me, baying like hounds after a fox, and with the same bloodlust that one might associate with that particular pursuit. The two smallest were terriers and they saw their role as noise and provocation. The two large ones were quiet but much more dangerous. They had the fixed, cold and pitiless stare of wolves. They had a mixed pit-bull look to them and egged on by the fierce yapping of the smaller mongrel types, they were closing in with a silent, deadly intent. They parted in practiced unison and came in from the sides. In thirty seconds my quiet enjoyable day had taken on a frightening edge. I was backing along the road, trying to keep my eyes on both dogs at once. I had nothing with which to defend myself. Later I was to reflect that I had been given advice on always having a stick, but I had foolishly assessed the risk as low. One of the little dogs, forgetting the things discussed at the team meeting, dived in for a wee nip himself. I aimed a kick at his head and he darted away to keep up his assault from a safer distance. This messed up the dedicated advance of the heavy cavalry and in the confusion, I turned and walked away. One of the big dogs charged into my back, hitting me high up on my pack. I staggered forward and almost fell, but managed to keep moving. I think, if I had fallen, things would have ended up very differently. I crossed a small bridge and looking back saw all four dogs standing on the road, having a debrief. They seemed to have decided I wasn't any longer in their attack zone, and weren't quite sure what to do next.

When I reached the 30km mark, I was only a few kilometres short of Kaiwaka, but the task for the half day had been achieved and I turned back for Waipu Cove. I had expected to see Joy by this time, but she was nowhere to be seen. I had run out of potable water and was starting to get dehydrated in the hot sunlight. This Otago boy was wilting and starting to get a headache. My mouth was getting dry as it often did in mountain ultras, when it was too long between drinks. In this condition I again approached the scene of the dog attack. A sensible, well hydrated athlete would have found an alternate route. He would have remembered the merciless look in the eyes of those big dogs. This wasn't who I was at that time, but I did make one sensible decision. I found a suitable stick, and like the Suess character in Solla Sollew, 'my troubles were going to have troubles with me.' Oh, I hear you say, he's a reader of the classics? Indeed. Another applicable line from that book:

'I watched out for trouble in front and back sections, by aiming my eyeballs in different directions.'

As I closed in on the scene of the crime, Joy turned up, looking a bit alarmed. She saw me marching resolutely along the side of the road, looking angry, with my stick held at the ready, and she thought this was about her lateness. I, on the other hand, was glad to see her, and thankfully drank litres of her great fruit mix.

She apologised for her tardiness. She had been engrossed in the Mangawhai Museum displays and the time had, quite slipped away. She thought I might like the museum too. She had been promised re-entry by the nice lady, without having to pay again, and she would meet me there in an hour. They had, apparently, a really nice café. Of course they did. Joy knew how to sing my song.

I did visit the museum. It was nice, as she had promised. So was the café.

I retraced my steps (sixty thousand of them) and as I climbed the coastal Brynderwyns again, the same traffic passed me, that I had seen in the morning.

It was dusk as I again walked into the Waipu Cove Camping Park. I had my 60kms and surprisingly 883 metres of vertical for the day. This was second only to the day climbing to the summit of the Desert Road.

I was tired but happy. Apart from the dog attack, it had been a great day.

### *Joy Leslie: Things learned on the Great March North:*

86. *So many things!!!*
87. *I am missing the brotherhood of motorhomes. These people in their campers have no idea when they see me in my – very tidy, borrowed – car, that I am one of them.*
88. *Rog walked through Mangawhai today and that means stream or river of rays. Te Whai - sting ray.*
89. *Our Covid test results came through as negative. Phew! Would have been VERY inconvenient if it had been otherwise. Thanks lovely nurse lady at Ngatea Health Centre.*
90. *That even though Rog was doing a catch up walk, it was still 60 kms and warm and perhaps some support would be beneficial. N.B. they held my entry fee at the Mangawhai museum and let me back in.*
91. *Was re- reading A H Reed's 'North Cape to Bluff' as research before we left home and he talked about the part that the kauri gum fields had played in the early history of Northland. It was interesting to see some and read about it at the museum.*

# Day 33

## Brynderwyn to Ruakākā

Day 33 began much the same as day 32, but this time Joy had to get up at the unearthly hour of 5am and transport me to the Brynderwyn Corner, where I had finished on day 31. The plan was to walk 12.5kms on SH12 in the direction of Dargaville, and return. This would complete the last 25kms of my deficit, and I could turn back North again. At the corner of SH1 and SH12 I got carefully out and set off very slowly towards Dargaville. Like the previous day's walk, this was a road I had never travelled before, so everything was interesting. It seemed in no time at all, I was passing the Maungaturoto Dairy Factory, which was a bustling hive of activity.

Then as I walked into the town I found it an interesting rural town, with a mood all of its own. The Kaipara Harbour was not far away and the town seemed to lean that way in topography and feel. Near the primary school, local Rotarians had created an area for children, called A Real Playground. I liked that, and might have had a wee play, had I not been so sore. At the school itself there was a sensible sign, which every school should have:

LOOK both ways and LISTEN before you cross the road! The Kaipara District Council should take a bow for this one. Consequently I saw no dead children lying on the road.

A happy looking fellow, driving the inevitable Ute, waved as if he knew me, but I was far from where I knew anyone. He stopped and came over to talk to me:

'Hi, I'm Tammy, I was doing deliveries in Mangawhai yesterday and I saw you several times walking along the road. I thought, 'what's that guy doing? He doesn't look like your normal street walker.'

'What does your normal street walker look like?'

'Without purpose, I suppose. But you definitely look like you have a purpose.'

So I explained my purpose, and as I spoke, his face lit up.

'That's amazing. I'm really excited to hear that. The government's treatment of the people has got everyone depressed, and looking suspiciously at their neighbours. Even ringing the cops about piddling things. Here's you just ignoring all of that, and walking from one end of the country to the other. Let me shake your hand!'

He gripped my hand in a fierce wrestlers hold that tried to convey months of isolation and frustration in a single handshake. When he released me, we both had tears in our eyes.

'How can I contribute?'

I gave him the flier I had and thanked him. He then escorted me into a nearby service station, and told the staff that anything I wanted to eat or drink was on him. I chose a cold bottle of drink, and asked if I could pick it up on the way back, in an hour or so?

I reached the 13km mark and turned back to Maungaturoto, which I understand, means mountain standing in the lagoons (or lakes).

Joy was waiting in a café called Tulip Espresso & Bakery. We had a lovely morning tea there and chatted to a few locals. One strangely eccentric character was wearing a lanyard with an official exemption from wearing a mask. He spoke for all patrons to hear that he valued his breathing too much to allow the prime minister to mask him. Then he took his coffee outside and proceeded to smoke by the open window, which we were sitting beside. Obviously, his concern for his breathing wasn't that great.

I picked up my bottle of donated drink from the garage, and was offered another to go with it. This was gratefully accepted too.

By mid-morning I was back at the Brynderwyn Corner, where Joy was sound asleep in the car, with a book resting happily on her chest. Here I met the theoretical me, that had been walking the 145 kms from Mercer. We shook hands, and I set off for Reinga alone. I was back on SH1 again. Apart from the 20kms from Te Hana to here, I had not walked on SH1 since Tirau. That seemed to be in another world, and another time, but it was only five days ago.

At the top of the Brynderwyn Hill I could see Whangarei off in the smoky distance. I could see Marsden Point, where we once refined oil, before someone in an office somewhere decided it was better for the environment to get someone else to refine it, then ship it here. The road down the Brynderwyns was as wide and spacious as the road up had been narrow and hazardous. The ladies at Kaiwaka had warned me. At the foot of the hill we took a small detour to visit a spot where one of Joy's uncles had lived. He had been delightfully eccentric and we had some good memories of visiting him there.

Joy was off to visit Waipu. She said:

'Toilet, museum, and ice-cream.'

Fair enough. I walked along the flat, and was delighted to see the Waipu sign stating that this was the 'Place of Men in Kilts, Rugby.' The mind boggled.

This area had a fiercely Scottish heritage. The settlers had left Scotland and gone to Nova Scotia, then thought Australia, in the form of Adelaide, would be better. Finding it was 'too sinful for these Calvinist types', they came here. They were either sick of travel, their wives refused to move again, or Waipu was sin-free enough to their liking, so here they stayed.

On the road near Waipu was a shop called Nutty for You. This kind of thing always took my attention. A shop for nuts, or with nuts, didn't matter.

The road along the flat toward Whangarei, was, to me, a bit boring. Just put one foot in front of the other and watch the traffic. The verge was wide though, so traffic was easier to avoid than it had been for days.

Joy was waiting in the car at Ruakākā School. Parked expertly in the shade. She was getting the hang of this stuff. The days were getting hotter. We had been invited to spend the night with friends Murray and Joy in Ruakākā, so the evening was great, in every way. Great food, great conversation, great company. Eating on the patio outside, in a balmy Northland evening. Murray and Joy had been, and occasionally still were, missionaries in Africa. They knew something of hardship, tough roads and adversity. It was so encouraging to talk to them.

Murray did some repairs and maintenance on one of my shoes. A stone had punctured the sole on my right heel. I thought I had a stone in my shoe and several times I took it off to shake it out, only to have it there again after a few minutes. Close inspection though, showed a long sharp sliver of stone had pierced the sole completely and I had a bleeding hole in my heel to match it. You might wonder how one could miss this, but my feet were so sore, a new pain was likely to be dismissed as trivial, until proved otherwise. This was otherwise and I had to remove it with the car key (don't tell Ian!).

Then the hole quickly filled up with new stones and I was spending more and more time with my shoe off, digging out stones. I was carrying a screwdriver from the car tool-kit for this task. I asked Murray to look at it, and after half his life on the mission field, he was an adept at bush repairs and improvisation. He filled the hole with some epoxy filler, and hung it up to season until the morning.

60kms done for the day. 25 to pay off the bank and 35 on SH1.

### Joy Leslie: Things learned on the Great March North:

92. *Shout out to the two different garages that we've visited in Northland. BTW. Garages are the best places when you're travelling. Not only do they sell petrol, but they have cool stuff like cold drinks, picnic bars and toilets. Anyhow, when the ladies hear what Rog is doing, they press free cold drink upon him.*
93. *Because Rog has been doing a bit of doubling back to catch up on the Auckland driving kms, he's had a couple of truckies who have seen him more than once, and had a yarn about what he's doing.*

*They're impressed with his purposeful walk and the determined glint in his eye.*

94. *I am a little concerned that I will be noticed also for my loitering with intent in available shade, as Rog does at least 10kms between drink breaks. Currently parked just outside a school, trying not to look dodgy. When I shared this thought on Facebook, my sister Cheryl advised me to lose the balaclava.*

95. *Museum of choice today was in Waipu, with a very strong Scottish heritage. Stern Calvinists, according to the displays, that had travelled here via Nova Scotia and then Australia. Another very well-presented museum – well done Northland.*

# Day 34

## Ruakākā to Pakotai

Day 34 started well. Murray and the two Joy's were up at sparrow's fidget, and the four of us had breakfast together before we set off. Murray brought my shoe out of his repair shop and pronounced it fit for the road. He thought it looked in better repair than I did. Probably a fair call. They bid us a fond farewell, and went for their usual walk along the beach, while we returned to SH1 where we'd stopped the previous day.

This piece of road had a lovely wide verge and I was well on the way to Whangārei by the time the sun rose over the Hen and Chickens. I was thinking that I might detour onto SH15 which runs parallel to SH1 to the intersection north of Kaikoke. I was told by a local, that it was only 3kms further, and much safer due to less, and slower, traffic. That sounded good to me, and I was sure it would, to Joy as well. It was roughly 10kms to the intersection at Otaika, and we met there for a break. As I'd supposed, Joy was all for the quieter road, and SH15 was nearer to her cousin Vivian, where we planned to spend the next night.

Joy went off into Whangārei to get supplies and fuel, while I set off up the Otaika Valley. It was quite lovely, and almost traffic free. I was walking away from the sun, and it was warm on my back. The occasional log-truck whooshed by with a cloud of dust and bark, but it was otherwise quiet. After SH1 leading into Whangārei, it was as complete a transformation as one could expect. The road threaded through bush, and crossed Otaika Stream several times. I met a few friendly chooks escorted by a magnificent rooster, pecking around nonchalantly on the side of the road. They were roadside veterans, and didn't bother to move when trucks thundered by a few inches from their tail feathers. They showed a mild interest in me, perhaps thinking I might be worth a bit of food, but soon went back to their philosophical pecking.

I passed a business called Doggie Doo's. Perhaps a distant cousin to Scooby. I wasn't sure about the correctness of the apostrophe, but I couldn't be bothered following that up.

Finally I came to Maungatapere (the meeting house by the mountain), where there was a small dog-leg in SH15 interspersed by 50 metres of SH14. On this intersection was a small eating establishment called the Office Café, and there, Joy was waiting, car in the shade, to join me for a light meal. It was a nice break. She had a new book by Maeve Binchy, so, in her words, normal service would be resumed when she was finished it. It was a nice day and I had plenty of fluids. I could manage. I read up on the town and learned that the stone walls I had noticed in the area, dated back to early European settlers in the 1840s. They were quite beautiful.

I was moving into dairy country and the smell of bovine was all about. Not just bovine, but dairy bovine, there's a difference. As the day wore on, I started to see cows heading in for the afternoon milking. One herd was moving through an underpass and they stopped to stare at the strange, brightly coloured chap looking over the rail above them. Cows, particularly dairy cows, are incurably curious, and have to see what's going on, even to the detriment of getting to the shed. My presence on the road may not have pleased all the herd boys I encountered. Our family had milked cows when I was young and the aroma of cow, still has the power to evoke memories.

Things long forgotten were bubbling to the surface of my fragile mental activity. Once when I was about thirteen, a dispute with my father had escalated into him suggesting that I needed dunked in the cowshed water trough. Filled with unreasonable confidence of youth, I had replied, 'Let's see if you can then.' The result was, we saw, and he could. I was never sure what the cows had thought of this.

These interactions with farm animals along the road, always had the result of having to start walking again and being reminded my feet were an absolute mess. I had once described the pain of losing our daughter, by suggesting I never got over it, but I got used to it. The pain in my feet was the same, and every time I stopped, I was reminded again. Every time I took a photo, every time I stopped to commune with a river and every time I stopped to chat with somebody who happened across my path, it all came back. I found the rivers particularly fascinating, perhaps I really was nuts.

As I passed the Poroti School, I was filled again with sadness at the silence. There is no silence as deafening as that of an empty school. It was as if some giant, political Pied Piper had taken them all away.

As I crossed the Wairua River, I saw a sign pointing to the Wairua Falls, only 2.5 kms away. I love a good waterfall, and I briefly considered making the detour. Briefly, that is until my feet joined the meeting. The idea of walking 5kms extra on a gravel road, was just too ridiculous to think about. I did make a mental note to get Joy to drive me there, on our way to Viv's that evening.

Then I came to Titoki and saw the Mangakahia Area School, named no doubt after the river that passed quietly through town. The school was quiet too, but it was getting later in the day. The bridge over the river was a long and narrow one, but the light traffic was kind to me and I made it across unscathed.

At Parakao there was a toilet with great artwork. Toilets were a point of great interest to me, especially now that we didn't have our camper. This one had murals of the logging history of the area. This was a relief.

I needed another 10kms for the day, so I headed off once again.

These last 10kms were usually the hardest part of every day, and this day was no exception. All my usual tricks to keep myself amused were wearing thin by this time of day, and it was just a hard grind. I made it to Pakotai, which also had a dead school, and called it a day. I had my 60kms for the day, and surprisingly 600 metres of vertical. We returned to the Wairua Falls and they were pretty cool, although I paid in heavy coin, getting out of the car to shuffle over to the lookout. Viv and Bob welcomed us to their home on SH14, not that far from Maungatapere, in the middle of an avocado growing area. Family fun is always special fun. Families say things no-one else would. 'You must be absolutely crazy to attempt what you are doing.' 'It helps.'

'What about Joy? It's pretty hard on her, traipsing after you, all day every day.'

'She's been reading a book all day.'

'Yes, but she can't relax, worrying all the time about you killing yourself.'

'She offered to do it.'

Bob was more pragmatic.

'Leave the man alone, it's amazing what they've achieved.'

'Typical men, always sticking together. I'll tell you something, if you were doing something like this, I wouldn't be helping you.'

Viv was secretly proud of me and Joy, but she had to get it off her chest. The two cousins had years to catch up on, and catch up they did. Bob asked: 'How much longer will it take to get you to get to Reinga?'

'I hope do it in forty days, so six more.' 'Six days? It's still 230kms from here.'

'Well maybe four days then, I'm getting 60kms in per day.'

He sat and shook his head.

'Sixty bloody kilometres a day. Jesus!'

### Joy Leslie: Things learned on the Great March North:

96. *The store at Titoki sells really great lamb pies.*
97. *A couple of things I miss from the camper - insect screening and, of course, the toilet. (Something to think about Ian, next time you are sorting a spare car).*
98. *Not many public loos on Highway 15. Store lady assured me there was one a couple of kms down the road. It was 12kms! Just*

saying. *N.B. it was decorative when I found it and functional. Both good things.*

99. *Accommodation the last couple of nights have been with friends in Ruakaka – thanks Murray and Joy, and a cousin on Highway 14. Thanks Viv and Bob. I hadn't seen Viv since the 1990s, but the whanau connection is there. We shared memories of our Grandad and the rellies.*

# Day 35

## Pakotai to Ōkaihau

Day 35 started at 4:30, as it often did. I'd have loved to sleep longer, and my frazzled brain certainly needed it, but alas it was seldom so.

Bob and Viv had said they would be up, but they were blissfully asleep as we had a lovely quiet breakfast. Bob had boiled some eggs the night before, in lieu of bacon and eggs, and they were greatly appreciated.

We drove quietly away and returned to Pakotai. Joy was asleep when we reached the starting spot, and I hated to awaken her. She looked so peaceful and innocent. I was envious of her rest. We agreed to meet again at the Twin Bridges, some 15kms away, and she drove off.

The Mangakahia valley was shrouded in river fog and surprisingly chilly. As usual, once my feet had warmed to the task, and I could ignore the damage I was doing to them, I started to enjoy myself. Being a creature of the early morning, my sense of smell and sound was greatly enhanced. Gradually the smell of the dairy farms dissipated and was replaced by native forest and pine trees. At Nukutawhiti I came across an old church, with rusted roof and flaked paint on the gate. The sign said, 'All Saints Church – services every three months.' The lawn was neatly mown and must have been looked after by someone other than the roof maintenance and gate painting committee.

As I was walking along the banks of the river, there was a sudden urgent sound in my ears. It was one I'd never heard before, and I looked around in alarm. Then a kōtare (kingfisher) dived out of the clear blue heavens and buzzed me again. It must have had a nest somewhere nearby. As a child I would often use such aggravated attacks to locate the nest, but those days were long gone. I ceded the battlefield to the little ball of protective anger, and walked away. I had never seen a kōtare do that before. Magpies, Stilts and Plovers, yes, but kōtare no. Joy was waiting at a carpark between the Twin Bridges. It was a picturesque spot with a river on both sides. She had set up morning tea on a picnic table in the park. A picnic table made of concrete. There must have been vandals in the area.

I had a little nap in the car, and felt greatly refreshed afterwards. Weirdly, I slept far better in the car at midday than in a bed at night. I set off up the Awarua River Valley and found it to be to my taste. The first few kilometres were all through native forest. The birds were singing and crickets were cricketing.

All was well with the world, until I came to a sign, on a forestry road, that brought some reality to my idyllic world. The sign said 'Trespassers will be prosecuted.' Someone had put a line through 'prosecuted' and added 'shot'. Probably a joke but for an over sensitive walker, far away from home, it made the hairs on the back of my neck, of which there are many, stand up.

I finally reached Tautoro, a small village in Ngāpuhi country. Joy was waiting on the side of the Road. She was buzzing because three people had stopped to ask her if she was okay? They were very friendly folks in these parts. A senior Māori gentleman was mowing grass on the roadside and came to invite us in for a cuppa. This was gratefully accepted. He said his name was Tam, and he broke out some carrot-cake to go with the cuppa. He was fascinated with our enterprise, and felt far too few people cared anymore about the mental health of others. He also felt the government lockdowns had made things a lot worse, and people were turning against each other, to the detriment of the whole community.

Then somehow the conversation turned to sheep shearing and he proudly pointed out that Tautoro was home to the Te Whata boys. Did we know any Te Whatas? Indeed yes. Samson Te Whata had been a folk hero of the Southern Shearing circuits when we were young. Tam said they were cousins of his, but not to get too excited about that because everyone was a cuzzie-bro round here.

We moved on only with reluctance. It had been a nice interlude. We had been shown a lot of kindness, but no-one had invited us in off the street for a cuppa.

An hour later I came into Kaikohe. I had been here before, as a manager with the Department of Corrections, I had visited the Regional Prison at Ngāwhā, just along the road, more than once. The town itself is the largest inland town in Northland and in the old days an important spot between the Hokianga Harbour and the Bay of Islands. Many battles had been fought here, and there were many burial places and small churches dotting the landscape. Hōne Heke, who made himself famous in Russell, back in the day, died here in 1850. I had a short break and set off northwards in pursuit of the daily 60kms. I fell in step with one of the seasoned citizens as I crossed the bridge over the Mangamutu Stream. The foot bridge was separate to the roadway, always a favourite of mine, and we exchanged pleasantries as we ambled along. I asked him if he thought the prison had changed Kaikohe? He thought it had, for the better. He said there had been a lot of NIMBY (not in my back yard) about the feelings expressed. He said people had complained about the four-hour drive to the nearest prison at Paremoremo, and thought it was unfair to expect poor people to drive this distance to visit a loved one. But when a prison was mooted close by, they all wanted it further away. Most people, he said, felt the prison had brought solid employment into the district and there were more cafés and restaurants than there used to be.

I turned up the hill back onto SH15. It was quite a hill, and mainly responsible for the 700-metres vertical achieved for the day. Over the hill I came upon Lake Omapere, and further along SH1 again. We were old acquaintances by now and I would stay with it right to Reinga. Excitingly the sign at the intersection mentioned Cape Reinga for the first time – 1900 kms walked, with no mention of the goal. There it was in white and green, waiting for me to leg it. Just over three days at the current pace. I could slow down and do it in four comfortable days, or speed up and do it in three. My feet said slow down, smell the Pohutukawa trees, but the head said go faster, and further. Common sense said the Mangamuka Hills were still to be climbed. The psychologists among you might be thinking I was showing signs of multiple personalities. You may be right.

We were to have the evening meal with Isabel, a cousin's daughter, and her husband Guillaume, then sleep at his folks. Joy didn't want to be late for that so as soon as the 60kms mark was reached, we were off back to Kerikeri, and a great evening. One of the great things about walking so far is the meeting and enjoying friends and family.

### *Joy Leslie: Things learned on the Great March North:*

100. *Last night was a very bad night for possums on Highway 15.*
101. *Gorgeous place to eat my muesli at the first rest place of the day. Twin Bridges.*
102. *Parked on a grass verge in Tautoro for the second rest place, and three people checked that I was okay and not broken down – mechanically and/or emotionally. The third person, Tam, invited us back to his house for a cuppa.*
103. *This is the town that Samson Te Whata, earlier a BIG name in shearing competitions, comes from.*
104. *Crikey, I've learned a hundred things, I must know lots of stuff.*
105. *There is a turkey in the paddock where I am parked, waiting for Rog to finish for the day and it's abusing me. Turkey in the long grass.*

# Day 36

## Ōkaihau to Kaitaia

Day 36, Sunday. So much had happened since the meltdown of last Sunday, it seemed like another life. We left before 5:30am. Joy had taken advantage of the fridge and freezer overnight and had a good supply of cold things in her chilly-bin. I drove, as per normal for early mornings, back to the spot we had stopped the night before. Turkey Corner, Joy had called it. There were a lot of wild turkeys in this area. On the way, we passed a road sign informing us it was 179kms to Cape Reinga. There was no talk of giving up now. We could smell the sea breeze. We could almost reach out and touch it. My dream, that had become Joy's nightmare, was almost over. What were three days compared to what was behind us?

Back on the road again, I planned to walk 20kms, then go to church back in Kaikohe. My step was more purposeful and the pain session didn't seem to last quite as long. I was now following the Waihou River which would run into the Hokianga Harbour. This was dairy land again and the only vehicles seemed to be milk tankers. The clear early morning air was occasionally consumed by the gobble of a distant turkey. I'd see one of the hideous looking creatures, close now and then, but they stayed silent until they had the safety of distance, before giving voice.

One distressing thing that marred my morning bliss, was a family of Pūtangitangi (Paradise Ducks) all dead on the road. It looked like a scene from post-battle Gettysburg. They are monogamous birds and pair for life. Once one had been killed on the road, the rest of the family hung around in solidarity until they were all skittled. There were thirteen of them. It seemed tragic that their family-mindedness was the cause of their undoing. Normally they would fly around me, peeping and honking until I had re-established what they considered to be a reasonable safety distance. This family would peep and honk no more.

Joy and the Strava app both agreed that the parking spot just before the Wairau Bridge was 20kms. So I hopped in for the trip back to Kaikohe. I was soon blissfully asleep, but my sweet slumber was soon shattered when she braked violently to avoid a turkey. A pox on all turkeys.

The folks at the Kaikohe Baptist Church made us very welcome. In this covid time, and particularly here in the far north, such a welcome was not always guaranteed. Among the notable things happening there was a gardening enterprise run by the church to supply veggies to the needy, and to deliver these by hand to reach out to the lonely. They also gave us a lovely donation for our cause. Good people.

After church we had a pie and some ice-cream to immunise me against the heat of the day. Then back to the Wairau Bridge to start my assault on the Mangamuka Hill. The day was now very hot and Joy gave me a good slather of sun cream before I set off. Ice-cream on the inside, sun-cream on the outside, thus fortified, I was off again.

Soon I happened upon the small settlement of Umawera. The school had brightly painted murals of sea creatures, appropriate to the area, and for some reason this made me happy. It looked like the kids had had a great time creating it, and it was outside. My own memory of school didn't have enough outside time.

There was still 10kms to cover before the serious hills, and I used some roadside change to purchase another ice-cream in the township of Mangamuka. There were good public loos there as well. What more could one ask for than an ice-cream and loo stop? There was also signage to Hokianga via the vehicle ferry, and I promised myself we would go back that way when we returned. Now I was thinking about things beyond Reinga, only 150kms away. This was a new thing. There was a time in every ultra marathon where you stop thinking of how far you have come, and start thinking of how far to go. You become attached to the end, rather than the beginning. This was happening.

Joy was waiting by the marae a little further along the road, with some welcome fluids. We had driven the hill before and remembered it to be steep and windy with many sharp bends. We agreed for Joy to wait where she was while I ascended the mountain, and if I deemed it to be too dangerous, I would call her for a pick-up. This turned out to be a stupid plan, because there was no cell phone coverage in the hills. In the end, she got sick of waiting and continued over herself. No doubt, picturing in her mind, my body lying down a bank with tyre marks all over it.

As I started up the hill, I saw in the distance a dog standing on the road. As I got nearer, he took on an aggressive stance, with raised hackles, that I didn't much care for. He had a hyena look to him. I didn't muck around this time, and found a good stout stick before carrying on. He disappeared through a hole in the fence and when I saw him again, he had gathered reinforcements in the form of half a dozen other dogs. None was as big as those I had encountered at Mangawhai but a pack of dogs is still something to reckoned with. I hoped someone at the residence would notice the commotion and put a stop to it. Alas, no such authority figure materialised. The original mutt was coming back to the hole he had used earlier, with the apparent intention of leading them all out onto the road. I took the initiative and, ignoring the pain in my feet, ran to the hole and arrived just as he was coming through. In such circumstances, a stick is a great persuader, and he decided discretion was the better part of valour. I dragged some brush into the hole, while he tried to stir the rest of the pack into a frenzy. It was slow work for him, because they had all heard him yelp. His street credit was in tatters. I walked rapidly away, before one, or all of them, thought of jumping the gate. A hundred metres up the road, I looked back to see three of them standing on the road, with the air of resignation about their collective demeanour. This one had got away, best leave it alone. Besides, he has a stick, that wasn't part of the original deal.

The road up the hill was as I remembered, but at a walking pace, much more beautiful. There were waterfalls and great forest giants hanging over the road. Traffic had picked up, being Sunday afternoon, but there were very few trucks. Usually I could hear vehicles coming and was able to take evasive action. I tried to text Joy, but there was no reception. Of course the phone never sleeps and when I was almost at the summit, I heard the ping of a sent message.

There was a great sign about litter, which took my attention, beside the summit parking spot.

Sadly there was also some unpleasant signage referring to the Prime Minister, and although I was no fan of government actions during the pandemic, this was quite horrible, and far beyond reasonable. I felt sorry for her.

In the end, Joy turned up and offered the standard high-quality food and drink, that I had become so casually used to. She reapplied the sun-cream, as I was starting to burn. I had been choosing which side of the road to walk on, based not so much on which was safer, but which was in the shade. Going down the other side was easier on the legs, but harder on the feet. There were large areas of road that had been recently repaired after slips and wash-outs. I was in awe of the magnificent engineering that had gone into this.

I had been wondering where the Te Araroa Trail (the Long Path) crossed SH1, knowing that it came down 90mile beach, then headed off across country towards Kerikeri. This was answered for me when I met two German girls walking up the road. They showed me their map and it turned out the Trail and SH1 were one and the same thing through the Mangamuka Hills. I had a good chat with them. They came from a small town in Emsland, that I was familiar with. This made them very excited, as they hadn't met anyone outside Haren that knew where it was. The world can be a small place. I asked them how they had found the beach? I didn't need to explain which beach, it was obviously still on their minds. They looked at each other and said they had almost given up on the beach. It had been soul destroying. I knew about the beach. I had competed in an ultra-marathon down the beach a few years earlier. It had been a hard day.

When I reached the Raetea Camping site, I saw where the TA Trail branched off again. I came back into farmland in the Victoria River Valley and followed the river down. I saw a banana plantation, near the road, where someone had posted a sign: 'When NZ becomes a Banana Republic, We'll be ready!' – I liked that.

We were planning to stay with Ruakaka Murray's sister Andrea and her husband Mike, in Kaitaia, so when I had 50kms up my sleeve, we called it a day. This left 125kms to go, with no serious hills. It was in the bag.

Andrea and Mike had a small flat, but out the back they had a five- wheeler caravan. It was a luxurious camper. My father would have described it as somewhere you could swing a cat without hitting any of the walls. We had certainly found a lot of nice people as we marched along.

*Joy Leslie: Things learned on the Great March North:*

106. *Accommodation blessings continue. Thanks Isabel and Guillaume and his folks, Luc and Catherine - daughter of a cousin, her husband and in-laws.*

107. *The abusive turkey from previous post, sauntered casually across the road with his mate when we were heading back to Kaikohe for church. Almost caused an incident. Brakes on hard - ruined Rog's post 20 kms/pre church snooze.*

108. *Wanderers are welcome at Kaikohe Baptist Church.*

109. *Quite a few areas with no phone coverage making occasional gaps in our communications*

110. *The Mangamuka hills are indeed steep and winding - and often without phone coverage – so Rog was a bit thirsty by the time I caught up with him. Next accommodation by whanau of the friends we stayed with in Ruakaka. Thanks Andrea and Mike.*

# Day 37

## Kaitaia to Ngataki

Day 37 got off to a sharp start, at 5:30am. We drove back to the Te Paatu Marae where I'd stopped the day before. Joy returned to her bed in the camper and I set off to walk the last 12kms into Kaitaia. A few hundred metres along the road I came to the Tarakaka Urupā, a local cemetery. I saw there the grave of Sir Graham Latimer, who had been described as the greatest activist for Northland Māori and Te Reo that there had been.

Sir Graham had been one of the original members of the Waitangi Tribunal and had once mortgaged his farm to achieve better outcomes for his people. Even though I came from the other end of the country, I had a lot of respect for this great man.

I arrived back at Andrea and Mike's place around 8.00am and enjoyed a meal of bacon and eggs in their kitchen. They suggested, if we didn't mind the drive, we could return to their camper that night as well. This sounded like a good idea and saved looking for somewhere to stay.

Full of fine food, I headed out of town towards Awanui. Kaitaia is a lovely town and I walked through it with enjoyment.

I was a bit nervous, as the threat of Iwi-run road blocks was still thick in the air. There had been one at Awanui, just a few days previously. I didn't want to antagonise local Iwi, but I didn't want to stop short of Reinga either. There was always the beach. Ah yes, the beach.

The road was wide with broad verges I could walk safely along, well away from the traffic. It was already a hot day, and I was trying to pre-load on drink. SH1 was a straight as a dart all the way to Awanui. There SH10 to Kerikeri branched off and so did most of the traffic. There I saw some council staff painting over some anti-Prime Minister graffiti. This made me sad and nervous at the same time. I noticed an old Māori gentleman sitting on a bench and I asked if I could join him?

'It's a free country.'

'Even so, politeness doesn't go amiss.'

'Tell that to Jacinda!'

'I've noticed she's not popular in these parts.'

'She came up here to tell us, locking us up was in our own best interests. Well, she soon found out what was in her best interests.'

'Still it can't be easy being Prime Minister in a time like this.'

For a while he just stared into the street and gripped his walking stick. Then he replied.

'It would be a lot easier if she didn't think she could lock us up like a bunch of criminals. They only care about the Far North when it's election time. Anyway, you were marching along like a warrior going to war, what are you up to?

'I'm walking to Reinga, from Bluff, in the interests of mental health. I hope to get there tomorrow.'

'Why don't you take the beach?'

'I've done the beach once before. I did the Te Houtaewa Challenge a few years ago.'

He looked directly at me for the first time. His watery old eyes took on a new inner light, and I could see reflected there, miles of unrelenting shimmering sand and blown sea mist.

'Did you now? I competed in the first one about 30 years ago. I was a bit faster in those days, of course.'

'I reckon we could still do it, you and I.'

He chuckled asthmatically.

'Make sure you treat Te Rerenga Wairua with respect. It's a sacred place.'

'I will.'

He tapped me on the shoulder with his stick. I wasn't sure what this meant, but I took it as a blessing, and left him sitting there, looking much happier than when I arrived. I was happier too. This, after all, was why I was doing this. I crossed the Awanui River again and headed on north. A lot of my nervousness had dissipated. Perhaps the old man had blessed me after all. We were fellow men of the trail, after all.

When I reached the Waipapakauri Hotel, Joy was parked comfortably in the shade, and as the hotel was closed, and it's boasted (rather than toasted) coffee was unattainable, we enjoyed a car meal.

There was a RNZAF Memorial nearby, and I grimaced over to read the signs. There had been a military airfield here during WW2 and this place had been the forward air defence for the country, when it was expected that an attack from Japan was imminent. The hotel itself had been requisitioned for airmen and had also served as a hospital. Waipapakauri means swamp where kauri grow. I could picture the giant trees dominating the skyline in former times.

Over the next hour or so I passed by hundreds of hectares of avocado plantations. Everywhere one looked there were avocados. I like avocados so I was happy with this. I could hear music rising from among the plantations as workers worked to the beat. Everybody was happy.

At Waiharara there was a butchery and dairy, all in one. There, one could purchase fresh meat, groceries, bait and ice. Another ice-cream opportunity. A notice outside said next Saturday, a line dancing group called the Far North Foot Fiddlers would be performing. Sounded like a lot of fun, but my feet cried out in terror at the very idea. I was also seeing signs for kauri gum-digger museums. This would be another must see, as we made our happy way back south, the day after tomorrow. I read on a commemorative plaque that over 20,000 people were involved in that industry in the 1890s. One could only guess what that meant to local infrastructure during those heady days.

I came at last to Pukenui which was a seaside port on the Pacific Ocean. From here one could go big game fishing, or any number of marine pursuits. One could even buy a paua pie. These must have been popular, because they were out of them. Regardless, we had a nice evening meal, before I set off again, into the unknown. Unknown, in that this would the farthest walked in a single day.

I soon passed the Houhora Golf Club which stated it was the farthest North in New Zealand. Who knew they even played golf up here?

As the day was drawing to a close, I had another dog incident.

white Bull terrier type, perhaps with a little Staffordshire, came running down a driveway from a house high above the road. He wasn't the barking sort, but he had an evil look in his eye. He ran past me and then moved to cut me off. This was unusual. Normally they were protecting property and position themselves between the aggressor and what they are protecting. This one was a hunter. There was something silent and venomous about his demeanour.

Even though it was only one day since the last attack, again I had no stick. I heard a car coming and this diverted his attention for a moment. In that window of opportunity I grabbed a small stone off the roadside, and threw it. I say small, it was perhaps 40cm across. I'm no hot shot at throwing, but this was a lucky shot and it hit him on the bony part above his eye. He gave a single yelp, and took to his scrapers.

An old dilapidated van pulled up, and the driver spoke through the passenger side window, which was down. It looked as if it was always down. I was expecting to have to defend my actions, but before I could open my mouth, he said:

'Bloody good shot mate. I've been wanting to do that for months. He's always on the road, that bugger, and the kids round here are all scared of him.'

'Well, I have to say I was a bit scared of him too.'

'Do you need a lift to somewhere?'

'No thanks, I'm walking to Reinga, from Bluff, and I have to walk the whole way. I'm hoping to make it by tomorrow.'

'Tomorrow? Shit, you must be some walker.'

'I get there. Thanks for stopping, by the way, I thought for a moment there I was going to end up all chewed on the side of the road.'

'Not when you can throw like that. Oh well, all the best mate, keep up the good work!'

'Thanks.'

The Strava said it was 66.6kms when I reached Ngataki. I had completed over 2,000kms. At the Ngataki School, a sign said the name meant: idealism, intuition, romance, generosity, creativity, wisdom and tolerance. I wondered how many of those suited me? Perhaps a little each of the last four.

Sixty kilometres left for tomorrow.

We drove back to Kaitaia, and the opulence of the camper.

***Joy Leslie: Things learned on the Great March North:***

111. *Kaitaia Pak 'n Save makes really good cheese scones*
112. *Someone in Northland has a similar taste in music. I could hear Simon and Garfunkel from a distance at one of my 'park and wait' places.*
113. *I read a sign in the pharmacy that said "Don't ask for credit, refusal can cause upset" so I didn't, and I wasn't.*
114. *'walkers on the road' are advised to look out for unrestrained dogs. Keep your dogs contained people!*
115. *On this road you can buy an ice-cream from a butcher – and he has much more accurate kms to the next public toilets info than the girl from a previous post. Toilet knowledge is always a winner.*

# Day 38

## Ngataki to Reinga

Day 38 dawned bright and mild. Actually it hadn't dawned when we drove quietly out of the park behind Andrea and Mike's flat, in Kaitaia, but it was light when we arrived back at Ngataki. Joy settled into the leather for a bit more shut-eye, while I laced up my shoes. Hopefully this would be the last time I would do it. Ten hours more and I could take them off for the last time.

Excitement was the main fuel on this day. My body seemed to be lethargic and my feet were dragging, but the call of the lighthouse was strong. I had never seen the Reinga lighthouse before, but I assumed I'd be able to see it from afar, and I starting looking northwards from mid-morning to see if I could catch a glimpse.

I came to Te Kao, in which was the last school I would see on SH1. There was one further north but not on the main road. The Te Kao School had a carved piece of Kauri for a sign which also said 'Kia Mārama' let there be light, or insight. A good motto for a school, but it had sad connotations for me, because this was the name given to a prison treatment unit for sex offenders. It was early in the day, but I was already fragile enough to cry over this memory, and some of the ruined lives I had encountered in that place.

The road now seemed to follow the contour of every ridgeline, and seemed to go to some trouble to keep that theme. If I could see a large hill off in the distance, sooner or later the road would veer that way and climb it. Perhaps SH1 just followed the paths of the old warriors, who needed to keep an eye on the countryside. At times I could see the two bodies of water to the East and West, at the same time.

Te Kao was where Te Houtaewa of the legend, had run from, down the beach. In the Te Houtaewa Challenge, I had carried a kūmara, on the great beach to Ahikara at the southern end, to symbolise a righting of the wrong. Indeed, Kao means kūmara, or dried kūmara. Beside the road, stood a white painted Ratana Church. It had the words 'Arepa' and 'Omeka' written on the two corner towers. I guessed this meant Alpha and Omega, and I looked it up to confirm that. I thought of the Alpha of my trip all those weeks ago in Bluff, and I hoped that the Omega would happen this very day. I stared off northwards, but still couldn't see the lighthouse. This was not surprising as I still had 40kms to go.

In a field to my left, I spied a large tractor stuck, with something like a potato harvester in tow. A part of my former life had been spent as an agricultural contractor, and I couldn't help feeling for the hapless driver. It looked as if he'd persevered a bit too long, in trying to make headway, and the wheels were well bogged. Another two tractors were being backed into position to give a tow, and there was a large group of 'helpers' standing around, not doing much, but seeming to be offering unsolicited advice to those still doing something. I slowed right down, because I wanted to see the outcome of this dilemma. When all was ready, the leading tractor took off, before the other two, and the tow line broke, with a crack like a rifle shot. I saw the line part before the sound carried to me, and the noise of the break was accompanied by some choice phrases of frustration.

The lead tractor was backed into position again, the line re-attached, and off they went again. This time all together. They were successful and as the whole turnout started to move, the group of onlookers scrambled up onto the harvester to do whatever their job had been. The paddock was wet and the harvester sank in a few more times before reaching the other end. Each time this happened, the main tractor would emit a cloud of black smoke, as evidence of the new effort, and this would be replicated by the other two as the strain came on. Also accompanying each traction problem, was yelling and yahooing from the team on the harvester. I loved the distraction, but it wasn't getting me to Reinga.

Around midday, Joy messaged me that she had stopped at a roadside café, called The Tin Shed. She would wait there and we could have lunch. This was very nice, although there was nothing wrong with the fare I was getting from her mobile kitchen.

Mid-afternoon I arrived in the small settlement of Waitiki Landing. This was on the Parengarenga Harbour. The signs warned that this was the last fuel stop in the North. Fair warning. Probably the last ice-cream stop too, and so I dug into my roadside change supply, as this would be the last chance to spend it. The day was turning out very hot and I had been lingering more and more in the shade. I purchased a coffee and an ice-cream to go. Both hit the spot.

As I set off again, I came upon the road to Te Hāpua, where the northern most primary school was situated. Then 100 metres further, the highway sign announcing Reinga 20kms. This was getting real. Less than a half marathon to go.

Around a few more corners, I could smell the unmistakable aroma of cattle. There was the HQ of the Te Paki Station, and the yards were full of milling black beasts, with steam rising from their backs. Men were working at the race and Utes and 4-wheelers were scattered about with happily tired dogs sitting, and panting in self-satisfaction. Everyone looked busy so I didn't try to engage them in conversation. The road though, was now liberally coated in cow manure, and I had to step with care. The irony of slipping and injuring myself on such material, was too much and I indulged myself with a good laugh. From here onwards there were several sets of stockyards and signs of recent activity. When I met up with Joy, she retold having a minor panic attack, when coming on a long queue of cars. She had thought the worst. That it was a roadblock operated by local Iwi, and that she would need to show her proof of Covid-test certificate. It turned out to be nothing more than some cowboys chasing bulls on the road. Quite the anti-climax.

I still hadn't caught a glimpse of the Reinga Lighthouse, but the anticipation was drawing me on. The road seemed to have more and more steep hills as I struggled northwards. There were great sand dunes to be seen, and even a sign pointing to the 'Giant Dunes'. One could even hire a surfboard to surf these dunes. No doubt a fun activity in normal circumstances, but my feet were in such condition that any activity involving feet, seemed to be on the other side of that great divide. My feet had been sore for so long I could no longer imagine doing anything but walk along the road, careful to avoid any camber, or roadside stones. I was even talking to my shoelaces, telling them that when I untied them today, it would be for the last time ever. They just smiled and didn't reply. AGRO the blisters sisters were still in full voice, but I had learned to ignore them. There was no conviction in their complaints. The lighthouse, where was the lighthouse?

And then quite suddenly, I walked into the carpark, heralding the famous lighthouse, and the end of SH1.

Tuesday 23 November 2021, 37 days and 95 minutes after leaving Stirling Point in Bluff, we had arrived. We had done it. There was no more road. Just the track down to the lighthouse, still some 80 metres above the sea.

There was no band, no cheering crowd of fans, no ticker tape. There was Joy and I, alone in the carpark, and Ian's car, that had done us so proud. We hugged for a long time, saying nothing. Neither of us had known what we had signed on for, but we had shown the resilience required for such a mammoth undertaking. I wondered how many wives in the land could have done what she had done? We had travelled through a country torn apart by government controls, unreasonable and sometimes illegal borders, and here we were.

I still had to walk down to the lighthouse to get closure on my quest. My feet cried. They had thought it was over. Just one more little stroll. 800 metres. At 1044, this had been the day with the second most vertical metres, second only to the Desert Road summit.

We took some photos, but didn't dally as there was a cold wind blowing. I hugged the signpost. I looked down at the point. At the Pōhutukawa tree growing tenuously on the rock at the very point. I could see why Māori revered this place. The great currents of the Pacific Ocean and Tasman Sea crashed together.

There was turbulence far out to sea, and in my heart too. I wondered what kept that Pōhutukawa clinging to the rock in such a wild place? Was it just stubborn, like me?

As we turned to walk back up to the car, I thought of the little boy sitting in the classroom, dreaming. I wanted to reach out to him, tell him it was okay to dream, and never let it go!

I think he knew.

### *Joy Leslie: Things learned on the Great March North:*

116. *He/we did it!!*
117. *Having our friends and whanau interested in what we've been doing has been a huge encouragement. A special thanks to those who have contributed in so many ways. Hospitality, the car, the give-a-little page and those who walked sections with Rog.*
118. *How to keep drink and food supplied and cool for long hot days.*
119. *Last but not least – to discern a good parking place from one not so great.*

# Epilogue

What does one do when the dream of a lifetime is realised? What is beyond Reinga (the place of departing spirits)?

Questions, so long ignored and put on the back burner of my mind, now had to be faced. We walked, very slowly, back up the track to the car. I sat down and untied the Hoka laces for the last time. It seemed another lifetime when I had tied them at Bluff, but it was only a little over 37 days. With my Swiss Army knife, I cut the bandages off my feet. Two of my nails stayed attached to my toes and the other eight stayed with the bandages.

I sat for a long time, and looked at the feet and the soles of the shoes. All four were in tatters, but had done everything, and more, that had been asked of them. I would keep the shoes as a memorial of the greatest task I had ever set myself. I guessed I would keep the feet too. They would never be the same, and it was hard to imagine them being pain-free again. I stood and looked southwards and thought of AH Reed all those years ago, setting off from here and heading for Bluff with his little suitcase and dressed properly in hat and tie (and good boots). I wished my father could have been here to see this. We have no way of knowing how long we will have loved ones about, so we need to communicate more often with them about our feelings and dreams.

Joy was close to tears as relief washed over her. Now she could have her husband back. Now we could do things together again, that did not involve walking northwards. We would travel back via the Hokianga

Harbour and that famous East Cape that had been such a dark shadow over our lives.

I was in a stupor of exhaustion, elation and anti-climax. Already my phone was pinging with congratulatory messages from friends and followers on Facebook. Tomorrow I would not need to get on the road at sparrow's fidget.

I had so many people to thank, I didn't know where to start. We had raised over $12,000 for ABLE Minds, and I was immensely thankful for this generosity, but I think talking to people about mental health had done the greater good. I wanted to give back to the community. I decided to sit down and write about the experience, as Mr Reed had done.

Maybe when I'm 85 I'll do it again...

# Appendix One

## A Walk on the Wild Side

I have often wondered where extreme athletes go when they disappear into the dark recesses of their minds. When they are running on empty, and seem driven by something no-one else can see. When they go far beyond the frontier of what one might reasonably expect a body to endure – and then, even more amazingly, return!

I have seen people suffering hideously, yet still moving, sails fluking with sparse wind while all about them are becalmed. I've seen too, helplessness and horror reflected in the eyes of their support crews and loved ones.

In the interests of journalistic research, I decided to go under cover and find out for myself. I entered the 200km section of The Great Naseby Water Race (GNWR).

You wouldn't describe me as an athlete at all, let alone an extreme one. I enjoyed sports at school but only because it got me out of the constraints of the classroom. This fact alone qualified me for the research, because in that word 'constraints' I found the key for unlocking the vault of the Dark Places (otherwise known as the Wild Side).

As I wasn't a native of the Wild Side, I had to apply for, and be granted, temporary residency. I learned their language, but in a heavily accented form that was easily spotted as alien.

Extreme athletes come in all shapes and sizes, with no external markings or gang patches to identify them. But all without exception chafe at constraint. They scoff at words like 'can't' and 'impossible' and eyes twinkle with inner light when someone refers to them as 'nuts'. When they come upon a frontier, they have to see what is out there and off they go, with only scanty plans for the return trip.

Preparation is the key to extreme endeavour, even for pretenders, so I did my share. I chose the GNWR because of its proximity to home, its looped structure, its beauty, its family-like atmosphere and my knowledge of the trail. I had been there before doing easy stuff like the 50km. Only in the rarefied air of Naseby would you insert the word 'just' in the sentence "I'm doing the 50km."

I actually trained for this and notched up a lot of kilometres wandering all over Otago and Southland, by night. The nocturnal fauna of Bluff Hill accepted me without quibble as one of their own as I puffed through their habitat up to six times in a single night. They would look at one other and shrug philosophically. I amassed enough headlamps to illuminate a medium-sized town and a pile of shoes that would have made any dumpster behind a shoe warehouse proud.

Most ultras have a drop bag system, allowing the opportunity to send things forward to be picked up at a future time and place. You have to put yourself into the shoes of the future and know what you will need and possibly how you will be feeling in that time warp. I once saw a girl take a note out of her drop bag which said in big black permanent marker, "Go, you good thing!" I thought, "Ah, how nice", but she read my thoughts and said, with some defiance, "I put that in there."

In the case of the 200 GNWR the drop bag system is in the head. I had to foresee the foray into the Wild Side and send drop bags for myself into the empty void. Of course one had to remember where they were and share this vital info with the crew. It's been well said that CREW stands for Cranky Runner, Endless Waiting and there are few places better than the 200 to see this played out.

The pre-race briefing with the 'CREW' went as I imagined one would before a Cold War spy operation. "The subject will be unrecognisable as the person you thought you knew. He will be sarcastic, intolerant, intolerable, impatient, uncommunicative, peevish, unrealistic, humourless, thoughtless and selfish. He will not care that you have given up your weekend to sit freezing in the middle of the night, to have things ready for someone who will grunt at you like a pig and may not even stop. If he does, he will probably only want things you don't have.

You yourself must be encouraging, reasonable, sensible, patient, gentle, and be a first-class mind-reader. You must also accept that anything that goes wrong will be unquestionably YOUR fault. At the same time you must be firm and allow no talk of quitting or doing shorter distances. You must not allow him to sit for more than two minutes and may need a stick or similar to enforce this. You may also have to follow at a distance to make sure he actually goes and doesn't double back. Don't, however, let him see you doing this. If you nod off even for a moment, he will return at that precise moment with a long list of unreasonable demands and make snarky comments about your 'level of commitment'. Please forgive me in advance for all this and see my walk on the Wild Side as a parenthesis in life that has no bearing on the real me! Later (after a few weeks) we will sit down together and laugh about the 'Wild-sider'."

And so the journey began. I strolled across the gentle slopes of comfort zone and into the foothills of hard yakka. I was constantly calculating time and distance and realised with sickening shock that at 80kms, I had used up well over half my energy but still was a good three hours away from half way. I realised too that the percentage increase of hardship per lap was rising much faster than the percentage decrease of laps to go.

I had reached the frontier. I could no longer continue to burn the fuel of fitness and athleticism. I was walking on the Wild Side. I was alone in the darkness. The wolves of despair that had kept their distance in the daylight, now closed in mercilessly with lurking intent. There in the thick darkness I found my first drop bag, a message from comfortable me, which said "There's no problem that will not be better in the morning (echoes of my gran) – make no decisions in the night!" I replied, "It's all very well for you" but I carried on. Later I found another bag, floating in the water race; it said "My heart will go on!" Jack may freeze and sink below the waves of nausea and despair, but I am on top of the wreckage AND I have the whistle! I saw other lights passing in the night.

Near, far, wherever you are, the void seemed everlasting. In the eerie glow of my LED light I started to see fantastic creatures. Among them I found another bag; it said "The monsters are not real!" One of them, in the form of Donny Trump, told me "Real heroes don't get captured!" As I tried to form a witty riposte, he disappeared in a puff of orange hair. Beautiful sirens were singing beseechingly in the night, trying to draw me onto the rocks of failure. They were disguised as warm places, comfortable chairs, food tents, friendly faces, somewhere to lie down and sleep (ah, sleep). Their songs reached out and caressed my self-pity. "Do you want to stop for a while? It's warm in here. Do you want some hot pumpkin soup and salty potatoes? Do you want your shoulders massaged? Do your socks need changed and blisters treated? You don't look so good, are you okay?"

Another bag; "Don't make eye contact with the sirens!" I stumbled over the last bag in the gloom. It said "The mind-numbing sleepiness will pass!" This seemingly simple advice was important, as I stumbled into one bit of trackside foliage after another and searched the sky for the crimson blush of dawn.

And then without really knowing when it had happened, I was back in the foothills of hard yakka. The sky was light. I was surrounded by other Wild Siders and there was banter again. I recalculated the time and distance and could at last see on the horizon the gentle slopes of comfort zone. It was on the far side of the finish line but it didn't matter. Even the foothills of hard yakka were now manageable. The path seemed suddenly well marked and foot friendly.

The crew had made me hot porridge. It warmed the cockles of my Scottish heart and infused my limbs with new vigour.

Because we spies don't take notes, we have to rely on memory to put together valuable reports. I searched the database of my mind and found out what Random-Access Memory means. While I had been able to send bags of information forward into the drop zone of the dark side, very little had been sent back. Little flash-backs of falling over, double-vision, wolves howling, tears, self-pity, hysteria and singing Elton John songs came to me in the pixelated video bites of a munted hard drive.

How would I summarise the mission? Great. Would I do it again? Absolutely! What was the take home highlight of the experience? One of Sirens and man can she sing!

*Roger Leslie (2018)*

# Appendix Two

## Hazard Mitigation

*The policy we must employ – for risky situation*
*identify the hazard and – install some mitigation*
*we register the time and date – and crucial information*
*and print it out (for auditors – and their examination)*
*prevention is the catchword here – before there's mutilation*
*(see: broken legs and blinded eyes – and finger amputation)*
*We will the hazard minimise – or put in isolation*
*and then as means of last resort – we'll try elimination*

*The H&S we have in place – is paper complication*
*the forms must be in triplicate – of trees the ruination*
*there's exercises, system tests – and peril simulation*
*the things we find to fret about – are most imagination*
*they're all recorded on the board – the health and safety station*
*the folders in the orange box – have added explanation*
*the only things omitted from – the danger correlation*
*were alcohol and its close friend – tobacco inhalation*

*To test a system working well – takes danger replication*
*and so we took a mortar shell – of army occupation*
*we hid it deep among the soil – and sundry vegetation*

*the dummy tester came along – to score an indentation*
*although he scraped it with the spade – it gave no indication*
*so marshalling the thinking style – that cursed his generation*
*he threw it to instructor Pat – for his examination*
*explosive was the terse reply – corrupt his exclamation!*

*he dropped it in his ofice drawer – reporting its location*
*which brought the army buzzing round – with bee-like agitation*
*they threw a cordon round the place – ensuring insulation*
*and took the names of those on site – oficial registration*
*they sandbagged in the ofice door – to muff the detonation*
*the outcome for the tiny shack – complete annihilation*
*but from the rubble Stu will raise – a new administration*
*how will, you ask, he get consent? – 'twill be an inspiration!*

# Appendix Three

## Running Through the Rainbow

*Oh Rainbow, Rainbow – how colourful you are*
*Your tapestry of shading – a canvas without*
*par to enter this was easy – at home I'm always bold*
*but oh the things I've suffered – to find your pot of gold!!*

*Oh Sedgemere, Sedgemere – just why are you so far?*
*It's 60 kilometres – more or less, by car*
*the driving there's a doddle – but what of running back?*
*I'm 'saddle' sore and weary – a walking blister pack!!*

*Oh Tennyson, Tennyson – your blue's a welcome sight*
*the poetry on shoreline – and valley cleft, you write*
*but ours it is to reason – in metre, word and rhyme*
*a light brigade of fragrance – in rosemary and thyme*
*I must one day return there – to smell the breeze and touch*
*with feet, these icy waters – when they don't hurt so much!!*

*Oh Fowlers, the Fowlers – what stories you could tell*
*Of diggers and their gold pans – and musterers as well*
*Of freezing mountain snowstorms – of candle's welcome glow*
*and halfway stage transition – of pain the status quo!!*

*Oh James, St James the Station — with river for a friend*
*like us, it runs and tumbles — as we the valley wend*
*your story like time's pen knife — is etched upon the gate*
*Another sweet transition — and drink, to rehydrate!!*

*Oh Hanmer, my Hanmer — I've longed for you all day*
*How green you are my valley — a picturesque gourmet*
*They say us mountain runners — are just a pack of fools*
*But they've not run the Rainbow — then soaked in Hanmer's pools!!*

Roger Leslie, 2017

# Appendix Four

## Wind in the Willows – Molesworth 2015

*Anticipation fizzed about – and rippled through the horde*
*That all the talk was fuelled by nerves – could hardly be ignored*
*The runners came in ev'ry size – were clothed in ev'ry fad*
*The only mutual feature was – the whole dam lot were mad*
*The station waited in the dawn – like willows in the breeze*
*The wind that howled across the peaks – whipped gravel round their knees*
*At last the bellow of the gun – cracked out across the vale*
*The birds which still had been asleep – took flight like startled quail*

*A dozen of the hardiest – set off into the wind*
*The ones with numbers red and green – on chest all safety-pinned*
*The chatting on the rolling flats – soon peters out and stops*
*They fight the gusty buffeting – anticipate the tops*
*The tendon burning starts to spread – and claim as well the brain*
*In scenery spectacular – they notice only pain*
*At last the road goes rapid down – a spiral zigging-zag*
*Of those who thought descent is best – the spirits quickly flag*

*The many drinks have taken toll – and now they have to pee*
*The hurt that threshed the heels and calves – is now in toe and knee*
*The aches and pains amalgamate – become a giant numb*

that emanates from muscles large – and centres in the bum
The laughter of the light at heart – and camaraderie
are swept away by ocean swells – of pain's relentless sea
As storms of dust tornado up – and flail the teeth and eyes
The wherefores might not come to mind – but definitely the whys?

The Molesworth is a mighty land – a 'stationary' place
that only those who live the edge – will ever dare to race
The hills could tell us many tales – of musterers and sheep
of athletes fast and furious – and those who sit and weep
of weather warm and tropical – where zephyrs sweet are from
of snow from off the southern ice – and nor-by-west maelstrom
We have to take her as she is – on her conditions strive
A victor in the Molesworth Run – is one who's still alive!

# Appendix Five

## Overcoming Barriers

*From the back blocks and the cities – humming ultra songs and ditties even
'scented' Rotorua in the North
From the mills that churn out paper – to this nutty running caper from the
bowels of Terry's shuttle, spewing forth
Via auto, plane and camper – chewing jerky beef and damper and no
outward sign of likeness could be seen
To the valley Ahuriri – battle worn and travel weary and they turned and
saw the vale where they had been!*

*Clearing spaces for their tenting – all the while their stress was venting
raking cones and other 'matter' sheep had sowed
Those that thought of ease and glamping – were reduced to normal camping
when their trailer ran (quite reckless) off the road
In this place of wild conception – far beyond the phone reception where
provincial lines were marked with turf and spade
Hear the happy girls that cater – with the hum of generator set the flavour
of the running cavalcade!*

*When they crossed into the Dingle – running pairs and running single
and the grandeur of the mountains took their eye
standing there they gazed in wonder – at the heavens they were under
and the treasure chest of colours in the sky*

*There was nothing to compare it – and on Facebook they would share it yes,
those slopes of scree that beckoned like before
Ah, but when they ventured closer – they would find the rocks were grosser
than the horns of Greece's fabled minotaur*

*From the Vale of Ahuriri – some with Roger, some with Terry
and the Barrier these runners would take on
While the wind flipped up their lanyards – they all tried to dodge the Spaniards
and the test was in 'voyage' (if not the 'bon')
While the tenting reservation – was transferred to new location
both the kitchen and the athletes wet their feet
See the demons of the doubting – overcome by mountain outing and the
smiles of satisfaction were complete.*

*See them cross the mighty river – melted ice of liquid shiver as they try to
read the current and the flow
With their arms all locked together – human chain of link and tether and
they wonder, just how deep this part will go?
With their legs of varied sizes – and sartorial disguises hear them argue
"Should we go, or should we stop?"
Whether tall or if whether shorter – whether Prince or whether porter their
endeavour was to keep their head on top!*

*On the walls is writ a letter – at the lodge they call the 'Greta' as they found
on there the hist'ry of the place
Where those workers of depression – carved their thoughts in deep impression
as they forged a road from Ohau's rocky face
Ah, but these the 'cade' of runners – were no beachfront group of sunners
so they took instead Ben Ohau's mountain path
In the Twizel streets arriving – at the summit of their striving And the
memory is sweet in aftermath!*

*Roger Leslie (March 2021) Apologies to Banjo P*

# Appendix Six

## The Taniwha

*The Taniwha of legend – infuses hearts with fear*
*and those who brave the river – may find him lurking there*
*The mists of early morning – disguise his scaly gaze*
*and lure the fool, unwary – to where the monster lays*
*A marathon of suff'ring – is waiting by the shores*
*for virgins of this running – and older dinosaurs*
*They stream into the forest – in happy single file*
*so far from home and comfort – these athletes of exile*
*In shadow of the Miro – idyllic running space*
*one soon forgets the monster – is native to this place*
*The birdsong of the woodlands – and flying water-fowl*
*can mask the sound of danger – and shield the giant's growl*
*The cold of early morning – around the river bays*
*is overcome with sunshine – and its relentless rays*
*Anticipation smiles – upon the lurking beast*
*He loves a salty runner – 'twill be a gourmet feast*
*As cramp of heat and distance – begins to break their hearts*
*yes, now the waiting monster – will bite their nether parts*
*As self-recrimination – is heard upon their lips*
*the Taniwha breaths fire – on weary knees and hips*
*He lashes with his tail – and slashes with his claws*

*and all the time there's roaring – and gnashing of the jaws*
*The blisters and the chafing – are taking now their toll*
*the Taniwha of legend – a 'mighty river' troll*
*But…… through the trial and suff'ring – the runners carry on*
*Unique are they in spirit – a super echelon*
*They one by one escape him – to finish line and cheer*
*and in his lair the monster – will wait another year……………*

Roger Leslie (2019)

# Appendix Seven

## She'll be driving to Reinga

(To the tune of '*She'll be coming round the mountain.*')
*She'll be driving to Reinga in the North*
*She'll be leaving home and comfort from henceforth*
*She'll survive on bread and butter, cause her husband is a nutter*
*She will criss-cross town and country, back and forth*

*She'll be driving in the camper when she comes*
*there'll be little time for sweeping up the crumbs*
*When there's water in the camper, well your socks and feet are*
*damper till at last in sheer exhaustion she succumbs*

*She'll be sitting by the highway with a book*
*She's ignoring all the others as they look*
*See her parked there on the shoulder, see her parking getting bolder*
*She's a driver, nurse, masseuse, and she's the cook.*

*She is nervous of the corners on the road*
*for her walker she is filled with dark forebode*
*And no soothing words will change her, as he puts himself*
*danger Yes, she wished he had a better safety code*

*See her cringing at the blisters on his feet*
*From those days and weeks of walking on the street*
*See her wade into the water, and the breaking waves that caught*
*her see her wet up to the armpits, in retreat*

*She is no mechanic as she drives along*
*"oh, come on, you stupid motor!' is her song*
*When that beastly thing is missing, for Samaritans she's wishing*
*and she knew right from the start, that something's wrong*

*She'll be dodging all those turkeys as she drives*
*And to find the best of laybys she will strive*
*When his smelly clothes she's scrubbing, or his bleeding feet she's rubbing*
*He considers her the best of all the wives*

*She has driven to Reinga, all the way*
*She can tell you that it's not a holiday*
*Yes, she lasted out the distance, she's a lass of some persistence*
*She has driven to Reinga, all the way!*

Milton Keynes UK
Ingram Content Group UK Ltd.
UKHW040818121024
449514UK00021B/28